Proverbs
for
Parenting

Proverbs
for
Parenting

*A Topical Guide for Child Raising
from the Book of Proverbs*

BARBARA DECKER

Lynn's Bookshelf

Library of Congress Catalog
Card Number 90-92206
ISBN 0-9618608-5-5

Lynn's Bookshelf
PO Box 2224
Boise ID 83701

NIV First Edition 1991. First Printing 1991
Second Printing 1992
Third Printing 1993
Fourth Printing 1995
Printed in the United States of America

To my children,
Jared, Nathaniel and Hannah

CONTENTS

Part IV   Control of Mouth

Part V   Relationships

Part VI   Wrong Doings

Part VII Godly Characteristics

Part VIII Prosperity

INTRODUCTION

One of the greatest things we can do for our children is to teach them God's Word. The words we speak help build our children's consciences, their understanding of God, and their view of life and the world about them.

> Deuteronomy 6:6, 7
> These commandments that I give you today
> are to be upon your hearts.
> Impress them on your children. Talk about
> them when you sit at home and when you walk
> along the road, when you lie down and when
> you get up.

Clearly, instruction in God's Word is to be an integral part of a child's daily life, and not something that is limited to a special half hour of the day or reserved for a formal fellowship.

However, even with this awareness, I found it all too easy to allow many opportunities to pass that could have been used to embed God's Word in my children's minds. Opportunities to teach godly principles of life were being forfeited and replaced by, "Don't do that," "Stop," "Quit," "Quit whining," "Quit fighting," "Quit arguing," "Be quiet," "Be still."

I realize that terse commands may not be eliminated and that they have their place, but these were fast

1

becoming my habitual response and a main verbal means of discipline and training. So, to help me replace the oft repeated "Stop" and "Quit" and "Don't" and "No," I categorized wisdom from Proverbs, God's instruction to young people, into areas that would allow me to utilize the proverbs in raising my children.

If one of my boys dawdles in carrying out his task of taking the silverware out of the dishwasher and putting it in its proper place, I have the resource and option of teaching him a proverb about work, such as:

> Proverbs 6:6-8
> Go to the ant, you sluggard; consider its ways
> and be wise!
> It has no commander, no overseer or ruler,
> yet it stores its provisions in summer and gathers
> its food at harvest.

And once I have instructed him with this proverb, perhaps later a simple reminder of the ant would suffice as encouragement. Or I could teach him:

> Proverbs 22:29
> Do you see a man skilled in his work? He will serve
> before kings; he will not serve before obscure men.

Proverbs 10:4; 13:4; 27:23 and 27 are other proverbs that will teach children the importance and benefits of work.

If my children begin arguing, rather than saying, "Quit it, you two," I can teach them:

Proverbs 17:14
Starting a quarrel is like breaching a dam;
so drop the matter before a dispute breaks out.

Of course in teaching this I would need to explain that a break in a dam may be small and only allow a trickle of water out, but that trickle wears away bits and pieces of the dam and soon ends with a flood of water escaping. Their arguing, the little verbal jabs and cuts they have started, should be ended before it becomes a full-scale yelling match and comes to blows.

If an older child finds himself envious, of what a peer has acquired through theft or dishonesty, he needs to understand that obedience to God holds the ultimate profit and gain for his life, and that God will reward us and meet our expectations as we reverence Him.

Proverbs 23:17
Do not let your heart envy sinners, but
always be zealous for the fear of the LORD.

A better football helmet, a perfect test score, and new clothes, are things we may desire, but one's integrity and honesty is more important than these. People who acquire things through dishonest means are *not* to be envied.

Proverbs 11:3
The integrity of the upright guides them, but
the unfaithful are destroyed by their duplicity.

The proverbs are categorized into many areas where children need correction (Laziness, Lying), direction (Control of Self, Control of Mouth), growth in godly attributes (Wisdom, Faithfulness), and instruction (Reverence for God, Trust in God). The table of contents gives a complete listing of these areas.

Certainly not every eventuality you encounter as a parent appears in the indexed topics, but within each topic are principles to be applied to many situations. For example, neither neatness nor unthankfulness are topics listed, but neatness may be taught from other topics given such as stewardship or diligence. For correcting an unthankful child the topics of happiness, greed, or complaining may be used. It would be helpful to familiarize yourself with the different topics.

Proverbs For Parenting will give you ideas for teaching God's Word to your child regarding many subjects. Obedience is a vital and rewarding part of our children's lives. From the topic of obedience, you may teach your child benefits of obedience. He will learn to walk safely, avoid poverty and shame, and he will be honored and become wise (Proverbs 3:12; 13:18 and 19:20). The grouping of scriptures by topic makes it convenient to prepare a Bible lesson on a particular subject.

I originally compiled these proverbs for my use as a parent. It is by no means an exhaustive listing of topics or scriptures on child raising. I trust however it is complete enough to help you as a parent raise your child in the nurture and admonition of the Lord.

As a parent you will benefit from *Proverbs For Parenting* as much as your child will. You too will increase in your knowledge and application of God's Word.

Ephesians 4:15 (Amplified Version)
Rather, let our lives lovingly express truth in
all things–speaking truly, dealing truly, living
truly. Enfolded in love, let us grow up in every
way and in all things into him....

In order to teach your child a proverb you need to
understand it. That may require some study. In order
to use a proverb in a situation you have to have it in your
mind. That will require memorization. I found that
by picking one or two verses from the different topics
to study and memorize, I was prepared to teach my
children on the spot.

We desire to see our children grow to be strong, pro-
ductive, resourceful, godly men and women. We need to
instill in them attributes built upon and from the Word
of God. May this collection help you make the most
of the many opportunities you have to teach and cor-
rect your child using the Words of Life. And may your
children grow and wax strong in spirit, filled with wisdom and with the grace of God upon them. May men
be astonished at their understanding and believing–the
unfeigned faith that first dwelt in you.

PART ONE

Reverence
for God

REVERENCE FOR GOD

Proverbs 1:7

The fear of the LORD is the beginning of knowledge, but fools despise wisdom and discipline.

Proverbs 1:29-31

Since they hated knowledge and did not choose to fear the LORD,

since they would not accept my advice and spurned my rebuke,

they will eat the fruit of their ways and be filled with the fruit of their schemes.

Proverbs 2:1-5

My son, if you accept my words and store up my commands within you,

turning your ear to wisdom and applying your heart to understanding,

and if you call out for insight and cry aloud for understanding,

and if you look for it as for silver and search for it as for hidden treasure,

then you will understand the fear of the LORD and find the knowledge of God.

Proverbs 3:7, 8

Do not be wise in your own eyes; fear the LORD and shun evil.

This will bring health to your body and nourishment to your bones.

Proverbs 8:13

To fear the LORD is to hate evil; I hate pride and arrogance, evil behavior and perverse speech.

Proverbs 9:10, 11

The fear of the LORD is the beginning of wisdom, and knowledge of the Holy One is understanding.

For through me your days will be many, and years will be added to your life.

Proverbs 10:27

The fear of the LORD adds length to life, but the years of the wicked are cut short.

Proverbs 14:2

He whose walk is upright fears the LORD, but he whose ways are devious despises him.

Proverbs 14:26

He who fears the LORD has a secure fortress, and for his children it will be a refuge.

Proverbs 14:27

The fear of the LORD is a fountain of life, turning a man from the snares of death.

Proverbs 15:16

Better a little with the fear of the LORD than great wealth with turmoil.

Proverbs 15:33

The fear of the LORD teaches a man wisdom, AND humility comes before honor.

Proverbs 16:6

Through love and faithfulness sin is atoned for; through the fear of the LORD a man avoids evil.

Proverbs 19:23

The fear of the LORD leads to life: Then one rests content, untouched by trouble.

Proverbs 22:4

Humility and the fear of the LORD bring wealth and honor and life.

Proverbs 23:17

Do not let your heart envy sinners, but always be zealous for the fear of the LORD.

Proverbs 24:21

Fear the LORD and the king, my son, and do not join with the rebellious.

Proverbs 28:14

Blessed is the man who always fears the LORD, but he who hardens his heart falls into trouble.

Proverbs 31:30

Charm is deceptive, and beauty is fleeting; but a woman who fears the LORD is to be praised.

STUDY GOD'S WORD

Proverbs 1:5

Let the wise listen and add to their learning, and let the discerning get guidance.

Proverbs 3:1-4

My son, do not forget my teaching, but keep my commands in your heart,

for they will prolong your life many years and bring you prosperity.

Let love and faithfulness never leave you; bind them around your neck, write them on the tablet of your heart.

Then you will win favor and a good name in the sight of God and man.

Proverbs 4:20-22

My son, pay attention to what I say; listen closely to my words.

Do not let them out of your sight, keep them within your heart;

for they are life to those who find them and health to a man's whole body.

Proverbs 7:1-3

My son, keep my words and store up my commands within you.

Keep my commands and you will live; guard my teachings as the apple of your eye.

Bind them on your fingers; write them on the tablet of your heart.

Proverbs 8:32, 33

Now then, my sons, listen to me; blessed are those who keep my ways.

Listen to my instruction and be wise; do not ignore it.

Proverbs 10:14

Wise men store up knowledge, but the mouth of a fool invites ruin.

Proverbs 10:29

The way of the LORD is a refuge for the righteous, but it is the ruin of those who do evil.

Proverbs 13:13

He who scorns instruction will pay for it, but he who respects a command is rewarded.

Proverbs 13:14

The teaching of the wise is a fountain of life, turning a man
from the snares of death.

Proverbs 16:20

Whoever gives heed to instruction prospers, and blessed is
he who trusts in the LORD.

Proverbs 19:20

Listen to advice and accept instruction, and in the end you
will be wise.

Proverbs 19:21

Many are the plans in a man's heart, but it is the LORD'S
purpose that prevails.

Proverbs 22:17, 18

Pay attention and listen to the sayings of the wise; apply
your heart to what I teach,

for it is pleasing when you keep them in your heart and
have all of them ready on your lips.

Proverbs 28:5

Evil men do not understand justice, but those who seek the
LORD understand it fully.

ROLLING HILLS COMMUNITY CHURCH
3550 SW Borland Road
Tualatin, Oregon 97062-9736
(503) 638-5900

Proverbs 28:9

If anyone turns a deaf ear to the law, even his prayers are detestable.

TRUST IN GOD

Proverbs 3:5, 6

Trust in the LORD with all your heart and lean not on your own understanding;

in all your ways acknowledge him, and he will make your paths straight.

Proverbs 11:28

Whoever trusts in his riches will fall, but the righteous will thrive like a green leaf.

Proverbs 16:20

Whoever gives heed to instruction prospers, and blessed is he who trusts in the LORD.

Proverbs 20:24

A man's steps are directed by the LORD. How then can anyone understand his own way?

Proverbs 21:31

The horse is made ready for the day of battle, but victory rests with the LORD.

Proverbs 22:17-19

Pay attention and listen to the sayings of the wise; apply your heart to what I teach,

for it is pleasing when you keep them in your heart and have all of them ready on your lips.

So that your trust may be in the LORD, I teach you today, even you.

Proverbs 28:25

A greedy man stirs up dissension, but he who trusts in the LORD will prosper.

Proverbs 28:26

He who trusts in himself is a fool, but he who walks in wisdom is kept safe.

Proverbs 29:25

Fear of man will prove to be a snare, but whoever trusts in the LORD is kept safe.

Proverbs 30:5

Every word of God is flawless; he is a shield to those who take refuge in him.

PART TWO

Wisdom and Instruction

FOOLS AND FOLLY

Proverbs 1:7

The fear of the LORD is the beginning of knowledge, but fools despise wisdom and discipline.

Proverbs 1:22, 23

How long will you simple ones love your simple ways? How long will mockers delight in mockery and fools hate knowledge?

If you had responded to my rebuke, I would have poured out my heart to you and made my thoughts known to you.

Proverbs 1:32, 33

For the waywardness of the simple will kill them, and the complacency of fools will destroy them;

but whoever listens to me will live in safety and be at ease, without fear of harm.

Proverbs 3:35

The wise inherit honor, but fools he holds up to shame.

Proverbs 5:23

He will die for lack of discipline, led astray by his own
great folly.

Proverbs 8:5, 6

You who are simple, gain prudence; you who are foolish,
gain understanding.

Listen, for I have worthy things to say; I open my lips to
speak what is right.

Proverbs 9:13

The woman Folly is loud; she is undisciplined and without
knowledge.

Proverbs 10:1

The proverbs of Solomon: A wise son brings joy to his
father, but a foolish son grief to his mother.

Proverbs 10:8

The wise in heart accept commands, but a chattering fool
comes to ruin.

Proverbs 10:10

He who winks maliciously causes grief, and a chattering
fool comes to ruin.

Proverbs 10:14

Wise men store up knowledge, but the mouth of a fool invites ruin.

Proverbs 10:18

He who conceals his hatred has lying lips, and whoever spreads slander is a fool.

Proverbs 10:21

The lips of the righteous nourish many, but fools die for lack of judgment.

Proverbs 10:23

A fool finds pleasure in evil conduct, but a man of understanding delights in wisdom.

Proverbs 11:29

He who brings trouble on his family will inherit only wind, and the fool will be servant to the wise.

Proverbs 12:15

The way of a fool seems right to him, but a wise man listens to advice.

Proverbs 12:16

A fool shows his annoyance at once, but a prudent man overlooks an insult.

Proverbs 12:23

A prudent man keeps his knowledge to himself, but the heart of fools blurts out folly.

Proverbs 13:16

Every prudent man acts out of knowledge, but a fool exposes his folly.

Proverbs 13:19

A longing fulfilled is sweet to the soul, but fools detest turning from evil.

Proverbs 13:20

He who walks with the wise grows wise, but a companion of fools suffers harm.

Proverbs 14:1

The wise woman builds her house, but with her own hands the foolish one tears hers down.

Proverbs 14:3

A fool's talk brings a rod to his back, but the lips of the wise protect them.

Proverbs 14:7

Stay away from a foolish man, for you will not find knowledge on his lips.

Proverbs 14:8

The wisdom of the prudent is to give thought to their ways,
but the folly of fools is deception.

Proverbs 14:9

Fools mock at making amends for sin, but goodwill is found
among the upright.

Proverbs 14:16

A wise man fears the LORD and shuns evil, but a fool is
hotheaded and reckless.

Proverbs 14:17

A quick-tempered man does foolish things, and a crafty man
is hated.

Proverbs 14:18

The simple inherit folly, but the prudent are crowned with
knowledge.

Proverbs 14:24

The wealth of the wise is their crown, but the folly of fools
yields folly.

Proverbs 14:29

A patient man has great understanding, but a quick-tempered man displays folly.

Proverbs 14:33

Wisdom reposes in the heart of the discerning and even among fools she lets herself be known.

Proverbs 15:2

The tongue of the wise commends knowledge, but the mouth of the fool gushes folly.

Proverbs 15:5

A fool spurns his father's discipline, but whoever heeds correction shows prudence.

Proverbs 15:7

The lips of the wise spread knowledge; not so the hearts of fools.

Proverbs 15:14

The discerning heart seeks knowledge, but the mouth of a fool feeds on folly.

Proverbs 15:21

Folly delights a man who lacks judgment, but a man of understanding keeps a straight course.

Proverbs 16:22

Understanding is a fountain of life to those who have it, but folly brings punishment to fools.

Proverbs 17:7

Arrogant lips are unsuited to a fool-- how much worse lying lips to a ruler!

Proverbs 17:10

A rebuke impresses a man of discernment more than a hundred lashes a fool.

Proverbs 17:12

Better to meet a bear robbed of her cubs than a fool in his folly.

Proverbs 17:16

Of what use is money in the hand of a fool, since he has no desire to get wisdom?

Proverbs 17:21

To have a fool for a son brings grief; there is no joy for the father of a fool.

Proverbs 17:24

A discerning man keeps wisdom in view, but a fool's eyes wander to the ends of the earth.

Proverbs 17:25

A foolish son brings grief to his father and bitterness to the one who bore him.

Proverbs 17:28

Even a fool is thought wise if he keeps silent, and discerning if he holds his tongue.

Proverbs 18:2

A fool finds no pleasure in understanding but delights in airing his own opinions.

Proverbs 18:6

A fool's lips bring him strife, and his mouth invites a beating.

Proverbs 18:7

A fool's mouth is his undoing, and his lips are a snare to his soul.

Proverbs 18:13

He who answers before listening--that is his folly and his shame.

Proverbs 19:1

Better a poor man whose walk is blameless than a fool whose lips are perverse.

Proverbs 19:3

A man's own folly ruins his life, yet his heart rages against the LORD.

Proverbs 19:10

It is not fitting for a fool to live in luxury-- how much worse for a slave to rule over princes!

Proverbs 19:13

A foolish son is his father's ruin, and a quarrelsome wife is like a constant dripping.

Proverbs 19:29

Penalties are prepared for mockers, and beatings for the backs of fools.

Proverbs 20:3

It is to a man's honor to avoid strife, but every fool is quick to quarrel.

Proverbs 21:20

In the house of the wise are stores of choice food and oil, but a foolish man devours all he has.

Proverbs 22:15

Folly is bound up in the heart of a child, but the rod of discipline will drive it far from him.

Proverbs 23:9

Do not speak to a fool, for he will scorn the wisdom of your words.

Proverbs 24:7

Wisdom is too high for a fool; in the assembly at the gate he has nothing to say.

Proverbs 24:9

The schemes of folly are sin, and men detest a mocker.

Proverbs 26:1

Like snow in summer or rain in harvest, honor is not fitting for a fool.

Proverbs 26:3

A whip for the horse, a halter for the donkey, and a rod for the back of fools.

Proverbs 26:4

Do not answer a fool according to his folly, or you will be like him yourself.

Proverbs 26:5

Answer a fool according to his folly, or he will be wise in his own eyes.

Proverbs 26:6

Like cutting off one's feet or drinking violence is the sending of a message by the hand of a fool.

Proverbs 26:7

Like a lame man's legs that hang limp is a proverb in the mouth of a fool.

Proverbs 26:8

Like tying a stone in a sling is the giving of honor to a fool.

Proverbs 26:9

Like a thornbush in a drunkard's hand is a proverb in the mouth of a fool.

Proverbs 26:10

Like an archer who wounds at random is he who hires a fool or any passer-by.

Proverbs 26:11

As a dog returns to its vomit, so a fool repeats his folly.

Proverbs 26:12

Do you see a man wise in his own eyes? There is more hope for a fool than for him.

Proverbs 27:3

Stone is heavy and sand a burden, but provocation by a fool is heavier than both.

Proverbs 27:22

Though you grind a fool in a mortar, grinding him like grain with a pestle, you will not remove his folly from him.

Proverbs 28:26

He who trusts in himself is a fool, but he who walks in wisdom is kept safe.

Proverbs 29:9

If a wise man goes to court with a fool, the fool rages and scoffs, and there is no peace.

Proverbs 29:11

A fool gives full vent to his anger, but a wise man keeps himself under control.

Proverbs 29:20

Do you see a man who speaks in haste? There is more hope for a fool than for him.

Proverbs 30:21, 22

Under three things the earth trembles, under four it cannot bear up:

a servant who becomes king, a fool who is full of food.

Proverbs 30:32

If you have played the fool and exalted yourself, or if you have planned evil, clap your hand over your mouth!

FOR BOYS

Proverbs 10:1

The proverbs of Solomon: A wise son brings joy to his father, but a foolish son grief to his mother.

Proverbs 11:16

A kindhearted woman gains respect, but ruthless men gain only wealth.

Proverbs 18:22

He who finds a wife finds what is good and receives favor from the LORD.

Proverbs 19:13

A foolish son is his father's ruin, and a quarrelsome wife is like a constant dripping.

Proverbs 20:29

The glory of young men is their strength, gray hair the splendor of the old.

Proverbs 21:9

Better to live on a corner of the roof than share a house with a quarrelsome wife.

Proverbs 21:19

Better to live in a desert than with a quarrelsome and ill-tempered wife.

Proverbs 31:3

Do not spend your strength on women, your vigor on those who ruin kings.

Proverbs 31:10, 11

A wife of noble character who can find? She is worth far more than rubies.

Her husband has full confidence in her and lacks nothing of value.

FOR GIRLS

Proverbs 11:16

A kindhearted woman gains respect, but ruthless men gain only wealth.

Proverbs 11:22

Like a gold ring in a pig's snout is a beautiful woman who shows no discretion.

Proverbs 12:4

A wife of noble character is her husband's crown, but a disgraceful wife is like decay in his bones.

Proverbs 14:1

The wise woman builds her house, but with her own hands the foolish one tears hers down.

Proverbs 18:22

He who finds a wife finds what is good and receives favor from the LORD.

Proverbs 19:13

A foolish son is his father's ruin, and a quarrelsome wife is like a constant dripping.

Proverbs 19:14

Houses and wealth are inherited from parents, but a prudent wife is from the LORD.

Proverbs 21:9

Better to live on a corner of the roof than share a house with a quarrelsome wife.

Proverbs 21:19

Better to live in a desert than with a quarrelsome and ill-tempered wife.

Proverbs 31:10-31

A wife of noble character who can find? She is worth far more than rubies.

Her husband has full confidence in her and lacks nothing of value.

She brings him good, not harm, all the days of her life.

She selects wool and flax and works with eager hands.

She is like the merchant ships, bringing her food from afar.

She gets up while it is still dark; she provides food for her family and portions for her servant girls.

She considers a field and buys it; out of her earnings she plants a vineyard.

She sets about her work vigorously; her arms are strong for her tasks.

She sees that her trading is profitable, and her lamp does not go out at night.

In her hand she holds the distaff and grasps the spindle with her fingers.

She opens her arms to the poor and extends her hands to the needy.

When it snows, she has no fear for her household; for all of them are clothed in scarlet.

She makes coverings for her bed; she is clothed in fine linen and purple.

Her husband is respected at the city gate, where he takes his seat among the elders of the land.

She makes linen garments and sells them, and supplies the merchants with sashes.

She is clothed with strength and dignity; she can laugh at the days to come.

She speaks with wisdom, and faithful instruction is on her tongue.

She watches over the affairs of her household and does not eat the bread of idleness.

Her children arise and call her blessed; her husband also, and he praises her:

"Many women do noble things, but you surpass them all."

Charm is deceptive, and beauty is fleeting; but a woman who fears the LORD is to be praised.

Give her the reward she has earned, and let her works bring her praise at the city gate.

JUDGMENT

Proverbs 2:1, 9

My son, if you accept my words and store up my commands within you,

Then you will understand what is right and just and fair-- every good path.

Proverbs 2:6, 8

For the LORD gives wisdom, and from his mouth come knowledge and understanding.

for he guards the course of the just and protects the way of his faithful ones.

Proverbs 3:21

My son, preserve sound judgment and discernment, do not let them out of your sight.

Proverbs 8:12, 14, 20

I, wisdom, dwell together with prudence; I possess knowl- edge and discretion.

Counsel and sound judgment are mine; I have under- standing and power.

I walk in the way of righteousness, along the paths of justice.

Proverbs 10:13

Wisdom is found on the lips of the discerning, but a rod is for the back of him who lacks judgment.

Proverbs 10:21

The lips of the righteous nourish many, but fools die for lack of judgment.

Proverbs 11:12

A man who lacks judgment derides his neighbor, but a man of understanding holds his tongue.

Proverbs 12:11

He who works his land will have abundant food, but he who chases fantasies lacks judgment.

Proverbs 13:23

A poor man's field may produce abundant food, but injustice sweeps it away.

Proverbs 15:21

Folly delights a man who lacks judgment, but a man of understanding keeps a straight course.

Proverbs 16:10

The lips of a king speak as an oracle, and his mouth should not betray justice.

Proverbs 17:15

Acquitting the guilty and condemning the innocent--the LORD detests them both.

Proverbs 17:18

A man lacking in judgment strikes hands in pledge and puts up security for his neighbor.

Proverbs 17:23

A wicked man accepts a bribe in secret to pervert the course of justice.

Proverbs 18:1

An unfriendly man pursues selfish ends; he defies all sound judgment.

Proverbs 18:5

It is not good to be partial to the wicked or to deprive the innocent of justice.

Proverbs 19:28

A corrupt witness mocks at justice, and the mouth of the wicked gulps down evil.

Proverbs 19:29

Penalties are prepared for mockers, and beatings for the backs of fools.

Proverbs 20:8

When a king sits on his throne to judge, he winnows out all evil with his eyes.

Proverbs 21:3

To do what is right and just is more acceptable to the LORD than sacrifice.

Proverbs 21:7

The violence of the wicked will drag them away, for they refuse to do what is right.

Proverbs 21:15

When justice is done, it brings joy to the righteous but terror to evildoers.

Proverbs 24:23-25

These also are sayings of the wise: To show partiality in judging is not good:

Whoever says to the guilty, "You are innocent"-- peoples will curse him and nations denounce him.

But it will go well with those who convict the guilty, and rich blessing will come upon them.

Proverbs 28:5

Evil men do not understand justice, but those who seek the
LORD understand it fully.

Proverbs 28:21

To show partiality is not good-- yet a man will do wrong
for a piece of bread.

Proverbs 29:4

By justice a king gives a country stability, but one who is
greedy for bribes tears it down.

Proverbs 29:7

The righteous care about justice for the poor, but the
wicked have no such concern.

Proverbs 29:14

If a king judges the poor with fairness, his throne will
always be secure.

Proverbs 29:26

Many seek an audience with a ruler, but it is from the
LORD that man gets justice.

Proverbs 31:8, 9

Speak up for those who cannot speak for themselves, for the rights of all who are destitute.

Speak up and judge fairly; defend the rights of the poor and needy.

KNOWLEDGE

Proverbs 1:4, 5

For giving prudence to the simple, knowledge and discretion to the young--

let the wise listen and add to their learning, and let the discerning get guidance.

Proverbs 1:7

The fear of the LORD is the beginning of knowledge, but fools despise wisdom and discipline.

Proverbs 1:32, 33

For the waywardness of the simple will kill them, and the complacency of fools will destroy them;

but whoever listens to me will live in safety and be at ease, without fear of harm.

Proverbs 2:3-5

And if you call out for insight and cry aloud for understanding,

and if you look for it as for silver and search for it as for hidden treasure,

then you will understand the fear of the LORD and find the knowledge of God.

Proverbs 2:6

For the LORD gives wisdom, and from his mouth come knowledge and understanding.

Proverbs 2:10-12, 20

For wisdom will enter your heart, and knowledge will be pleasant to your soul.

Discretion will protect you, and understanding will guard you.

Wisdom will save you from the ways of wicked men, from men whose words are perverse,

Thus you will walk in the ways of good men and keep to the paths of the righteous.

Proverbs 5:1, 2

My son, pay attention to my wisdom, listen well to my words of insight,

that you may maintain discretion and your lips may preserve knowledge.

Proverbs 8:5, 6

You who are simple, gain prudence; you who are foolish, gain understanding.

Listen, for I have worthy things to say; I open my lips to speak what is right.

Proverbs 8:10

Choose my instruction instead of silver, knowledge rather than choice gold.

Proverbs 8:12

I, wisdom, dwell together with prudence; I possess knowledge and discretion.

Proverbs 9:10

The fear of the LORD is the beginning of wisdom, and knowledge of the Holy One is understanding.

Proverbs 9:13

The woman Folly is loud; she is undisciplined and without knowledge.

Proverbs 10:14

Wise men store up knowledge, but the mouth of a fool invites ruin.

Proverbs 11:9

With his mouth the godless destroys his neighbor, but through knowledge the righteous escape.

Proverbs 12:1

Whoever loves discipline loves knowledge, but he who hates correction is stupid.

Proverbs 12:23

A prudent man keeps his knowledge to himself, but the heart of fools blurts out folly.

Proverbs 13:16

Every prudent man acts out of knowledge, but a fool exposes his folly.

Proverbs 14:6

The mocker seeks wisdom and finds none, but knowledge comes easily to the discerning.

Proverbs 14:7

Stay away from a foolish man, for you will not find knowledge on his lips.

Proverbs 14:15

A simple man believes anything, but a prudent man gives thought to his steps.

Proverbs 14:18

The simple inherit folly, but the prudent are crowned with knowledge.

Proverbs 15:2

The tongue of the wise commends knowledge, but the mouth of the fool gushes folly.

Proverbs 15:7

The lips of the wise spread knowledge; not so the hearts of
fools.

Proverbs 15:14

The discerning heart seeks knowledge, but the mouth of a
fool feeds on folly.

Proverbs 17:27

A man of knowledge uses words with restraint, and a man
of understanding is even-tempered.

Proverbs 18:1

An unfriendly man pursues selfish ends; he defies all sound
judgment.

Proverbs 18:15

The heart of the discerning acquires knowledge; the ears of
the wise seek it out.

Proverbs 19:2

It is not good to have zeal without knowledge, nor to be
hasty and miss the way.

Proverbs 19:25

Flog a mocker, and the simple will learn prudence; rebuke a
discerning man, and he will gain knowledge.

Proverbs 19:27

Stop listening to instruction, my son, and you will stray
from the words of knowledge.

Proverbs 20:15

Gold there is, and rubies in abundance, but lips that speak
knowledge are a rare jewel.

Proverbs 21:11

When a mocker is punished, the simple gain wisdom; when
a wise man is instructed, he gets knowledge.

Proverbs 22:12

The eyes of the LORD keep watch over knowledge, but he
frustrates the words of the unfaithful.

Proverbs 23:12

Apply your heart to instruction and your ears to words of
knowledge.

Proverbs 24:3, 4

By wisdom a house is built, and through understanding it is
established;

through knowledge its rooms are filled with rare and
beautiful treasures.

Proverbs 24:5

A wise man has great power, and a man of knowledge increases strength.

Proverbs 28:2

When a country is rebellious, it has many rulers, but a man of understanding and knowledge maintains order.

MARRIAGE AND SEX

Proverbs 2:10, 16-19

For wisdom will enter your heart, and knowledge will be pleasant to your soul.

It will save you also from the adulteress, from the wayward wife with her seductive words,

who has left the partner of her youth and ignored the covenant she made before God.

For her house leads down to death and her paths to the spirits of the dead.

None who go to her return or attain the paths of life.

Proverbs 5:3-21

For the lips of an adulteress drip honey, and her speech is smoother than oil;

but in the end she is bitter as gall, sharp as a double-edged sword.

Her feet go down to death; her steps lead straight to the grave.

She gives no thought to the way of life; her paths are crooked, but she knows it not.

Now then, my sons, listen to me; do not turn aside from what I say.

Keep to a path far from her, do not go near the door of her house,

lest you give your best strength to others and your years to one who is cruel,

lest strangers feast on your wealth and your toil enrich another man's house.

At the end of your life you will groan, when your flesh and body are spent.

You will say, "How I hated discipline! How my heart spurned correction!

I would not obey my teachers or listen to my instructors.

I have come to the brink of utter ruin in the midst of the whole assembly."

Drink water from your own cistern, running water from your own well.

Should your springs overflow in the streets, your streams of water in the public squares?

Let them be yours alone, never to be shared with strangers.

May your fountain be blessed, and may you rejoice in the wife of your youth.

A loving doe, a graceful deer--may her breasts satisfy you always, may you ever be captivated by her love.

Why be captivated, my son, by an adulteress? Why embrace the bosom of another man's wife?

For a man's ways are in full view of the LORD, and he examines all his paths.

Proverbs 6:23-35

For these commands are a lamp, this teaching is a light, and the corrections of discipline are the way to life,

Keeping you from the immoral woman, from the smooth tongue of the wayward wife.

Do not lust in your heart after her beauty or let her captivate you with her eyes,

for the prostitute reduces you to a loaf of bread, and the adulteress preys upon your very life.

Can a man scoop fire into his lap without his clothes being burned?

Can a man walk on hot coals without his feet being scorched?

So is he who sleeps with another man's wife; no one who touches her will go unpunished.

Men do not despise a thief if he steals to satisfy his hunger when he is starving.

Yet if he is caught, he must pay sevenfold, though it costs him all the wealth of his house.

But a man who commits adultery lacks judgment; whoever does so destroys himself.

Blows and disgrace are his lot, and his shame will never be wiped away;

for jealousy arouses a husband's fury, and he will show no mercy when he takes revenge.

He will not accept any compensation; he will refuse the bribe, however great it is.

Proverbs 7:1-27

My son, keep my words and store up my commands within you.

Keep my commands and you will live; guard my teachings as the apple of your eye.

Bind them on your fingers; write them on the tablet of your heart.

Say to wisdom, "You are my sister," and call understanding your kinsman;

they will keep you from the adulteress, from the wayward wife with her seductive words.

At the window of my house I looked out through the lattice.

I saw among the simple, I noticed among the young men, a youth who lacked judgment.

He was going down the street near her corner, walking along in the direction of her house

at twilight, as the day was fading, as the dark of night set in.

Then out came a woman to meet him, dressed like a prostitute and with crafty intent.

(She is loud and defiant, her feet never stay at home;

now in the street, now in the squares, at every corner she lurks.)

She took hold of him and kissed him and with a brazen face she said:

"I have fellowship offerings at home; today I fulfilled my vows.

So I came out to meet you; I looked for you and have found you!

I have covered my bed with colored linens from Egypt.

I have perfumed my bed with myrrh, aloes and cinnamon.

Come, let's drink deep of love till morning; let's enjoy ourselves with love!

My husband is not at home; he has gone on a long journey.

He took his purse filled with money and will not be home till full moon."

With persuasive words she led him astray; she seduced him with her smooth talk.

All at once he followed her like an ox going to the slaughter, like a deer stepping into a noose

till an arrow pierces his liver, like a bird darting into a snare, little knowing it will cost him his life.

Now then, my sons, listen to me; pay attention to what I say.

Do not let your heart turn to her ways or stray into her paths.

Many are the victims she has brought down; her slain are a mighty throng.

Her house is a highway to the grave, leading down to the chambers of death.

Proverbs 9:13-18

The woman Folly is loud; she is undisciplined and without knowledge.

She sits at the door of her house, on a seat at the highest point of the city,

calling out to those who pass by, who go straight on their way.

"Let all who are simple come in here!" she says to those who lack judgment.

"Stolen water is sweet; food eaten in secret is delicious!"

But little do they know that the dead are there, that her guests are in the depths of the grave.

Proverbs 12:4

A wife of noble character is her husband's crown, but a disgraceful wife is like decay in his bones.

Proverbs 14:1

The wise woman builds her house, but with her own hands the foolish one tears hers down.

Proverbs 17:1

Better a dry crust with peace and quiet than a house full of feasting, with strife.

Proverbs 18:22

He who finds a wife finds what is good and receives favor from the LORD.

Proverbs 19:13

A foolish son is his father's ruin, and a quarrelsome wife is like a constant dripping.

Proverbs 19:14

Houses and wealth are inherited from parents, but a prudent wife is from the LORD.

Proverbs 21:9

Better to live on a corner of the roof than share a house with a quarrelsome wife.

Proverbs 22:14

The mouth of an adulteress is a deep pit; he who is under the LORD'S wrath will fall into it.

Proverbs 23:26-28

My son, give me your heart and let your eyes keep to my ways,

for a prostitute is a deep pit and a wayward wife is a narrow well.

Like a bandit she lies in wait, and multiplies the unfaithful among men.

Proverbs 29:3

A man who loves wisdom brings joy to his father, but a companion of prostitutes squanders his wealth.

Proverbs 30:18, 19

There are three things that are too amazing for me, four that I do not understand:

the way of an eagle in the sky, the way of a snake on a rock, the way of a ship on the high seas, and the way of a man with a maiden.

Proverbs 30:20

This is the way of an adulteress: She eats and wipes her mouth and says, 'I've done nothing wrong.'

Proverbs 30:21, 23

Under three things the earth trembles, under four it cannot bear up:

an unloved woman who is married, and a maidservant who displaces her mistress.

Proverbs 31:3

Do not spend your strength on women, your vigor on those who ruin kings.

Proverbs 31:10, 11, 28

A wife of noble character who can find? She is worth far more than rubies.

Her husband has full confidence in her and lacks nothing of value.

Her children arise and call her blessed; her husband also, and he praises her:

OBEDIENCE

Proverbs 1:5

Let the wise listen and add to their learning, and let the discerning get guidance.

Proverbs 1:8, 9

Listen, my son, to your father's instruction and do not forsake your mother's teaching.

They will be a garland to grace your head and a chain to adorn your neck.

Proverbs 2:1-9

My son, if you accept my words and store up my commands within you,

turning your ear to wisdom and applying your heart to understanding,

and if you call out for insight and cry aloud for understanding,

and if you look for it as for silver and search for it as for hidden treasure,

then you will understand the fear of the LORD and find the knowledge of God.

For the LORD gives wisdom, and from his mouth come knowledge and understanding.

He holds victory in store for the upright, he is a shield to those whose walk is blameless,

for he guards the course of the just and protects the way of his faithful ones.

Then you will understand what is right and just and fair-- every good path.

Proverbs 3:1-4

My son, do not forget my teaching, but keep my commands in your heart,

for they will prolong your life many years and bring you prosperity.

Let love and faithfulness never leave you; bind them around your neck, write them on the tablet of your heart.

Then you will win favor and a good name in the sight of God and man.

Proverbs 3:21-24

My son, preserve sound judgment and discernment, do not let them out of your sight;

they will be life for you, an ornament to grace your neck.

Then you will go on your way in safety, and your foot will not stumble;

when you lie down, you will not be afraid; when you lie down, your sleep will be sweet.

Proverbs 4:1-5

Listen, my sons, to a father's instruction; pay attention and gain understanding.

I give you sound learning, so do not forsake my teaching.

When I was a boy in my father's house, still tender, and an only child of my mother,

he taught me and said, "Lay hold of my words with all your heart; keep my commands and you will live.

Get wisdom, get understanding; do not forget my words or swerve from them."

Proverbs 4:10

Listen, my son, accept what I say, and the years of your life will be many.

Proverbs 4:13

Hold on to instruction, do not let it go; guard it well, for it is your life.

Proverbs 4:20-22

My son, pay attention to what I say; listen closely to my words.

Do not let them out of your sight, keep them within your heart;

for they are life to those who find them and health to a man's whole body.

Proverbs 5:1, 2

My son, pay attention to my wisdom, listen well to my words of insight,

that you may maintain discretion and your lips may preserve knowledge.

Proverbs 6:20-23

My son, keep your father's commands and do not forsake your mother's teaching.

Bind them upon your heart forever; fasten them around your neck.

When you walk, they will guide you; when you sleep, they will watch over you; when you awake, they will speak to you.

For these commands are a lamp, this teaching is a light, and the corrections of discipline are the way to life.

Proverbs 7:1-3

My son, keep my words and store up my commands within you.

Keep my commands and you will live; guard my teachings as the apple of your eye.

Bind them on your fingers; write them on the tablet of your heart.

Proverbs 8:32-36

"Now then, my sons, listen to me; blessed are those who keep my ways.

Listen to my instruction and be wise; do not ignore it.

Blessed is the man who listens to me, watching daily at my doors, waiting at my doorway.

For whoever finds me finds life and receives favor from the LORD.

But whoever fails to find me harms himself; all who hate me love death."

Proverbs 9:9

Instruct a wise man and he will be wiser still; teach a righteous man and he will add to his learning.

Proverbs 10:8

The wise in heart accept commands, but a chattering fool comes to ruin.

Proverbs 10:17

He who heeds discipline shows the way to life, but whoever ignores correction leads others astray.

Proverbs 12:1

Whoever loves discipline loves knowledge, but he who hates correction is stupid.

Proverbs 12:15

The way of a fool seems right to him, but a wise man listens to advice.

Proverbs 13:1

A wise son heeds his father's instruction, but a mocker does not listen to rebuke.

Proverbs 13:18

He who ignores discipline comes to poverty and shame, but whoever heeds correction is honored.

Proverbs 15:5

A fool spurns his father's discipline, but whoever heeds correction shows prudence.

Proverbs 15:32

He who ignores discipline despises himself, but whoever heeds correction gains understanding.

Proverbs 19:16

He who obeys instructions guards his life, but he who is contemptuous of his ways will die.

Proverbs 19:20

Listen to advice and accept instruction, and in the end you will be wise.

Proverbs 21:11

When a mocker is punished, the simple gain wisdom; when a wise man is instructed, he gets knowledge.

Proverbs 22:17, 18

Pay attention and listen to the sayings of the wise; apply your heart to what I teach,

for it is pleasing when you keep them in your heart and have all of them ready on your lips.

Proverbs 23:19, 22

Listen, my son, and be wise, and keep your heart on the right path.

Listen to your father, who gave you life, and do not despise your mother when she is old.

Proverbs 28:7

He who keeps the law is a discerning son, but a companion of gluttons disgraces his father.

Proverbs 29:18

Where there is no revelation, the people cast off restraint; but blessed is he who keeps the law.

Proverbs 30:17
The eye that mocks a father, that scorns obedience to a mother, will be pecked out by the ravens of the valley, will be eaten by the vultures.

REPROOF AND CORRECTION

Proverbs 1:20, 23, 25, 26

Wisdom calls aloud in the street, she raises her voice in the public squares;

If you had responded to my rebuke, I would have poured out my heart to you and made my thoughts known to you.

since you ignored all my advice and would not accept my rebuke,

I in turn will laugh at your disaster; I will mock when calamity overtakes you.

Proverbs 1:29-33

Since they hated knowledge and did not choose to fear the LORD,

since they would not accept my advice and spurned my rebuke,

they will eat the fruit of their ways and be filled with the fruit of their schemes.

For the waywardness of the simple will kill them, and the complacency of fools will destroy them;

but whoever listens to me will live in safety and be at ease, without fear of harm.

Proverbs 3:11, 12

My son, do not despise the LORD'S discipline and do not resent his rebuke,

because the LORD disciplines those he loves, as a father the son he delights in.

Proverbs 6:23

For these commands are a lamp, this teaching is a light, and the corrections of discipline are the way to life.

Proverbs 9:8

Do not rebuke a mocker or he will hate you; rebuke a wise man and he will love you.

Proverbs 10:17

He who heeds discipline shows the way to life, but whoever ignores correction leads others astray.

Proverbs 12:1

Whoever loves discipline loves knowledge, but he who hates correction is stupid.

Proverbs 13:1

A wise son heeds his father's instruction, but a mocker does not listen to rebuke.

Proverbs 13:13

He who scorns instruction will pay for it, but he who respects a command is rewarded.

Proverbs 13:18

He who ignores discipline comes to poverty and shame, but whoever heeds correction is honored.

Proverbs 13:24

He who spares the rod hates his son, but he who loves him is careful to discipline him.

Proverbs 15:5

A fool spurns his father's discipline, but whoever heeds correction shows prudence.

Proverbs 15:10

Stern discipline awaits him who leaves the path; he who hates correction will die.

Proverbs 15:12

A mocker resents correction; he will not consult the wise.

Proverbs 15:31

He who listens to a life-giving rebuke will be at home among the wise.

Proverbs 15:32

He who ignores discipline despises himself, but whoever heeds correction gains understanding.

Proverbs 17:10

A rebuke impresses a man of discernment more than a hundred lashes a fool.

Proverbs 19:18

Discipline your son, for in that there is hope; do not be a willing party to his death.

Proverbs 19:25

Flog a mocker, and the simple will learn prudence; rebuke a discerning man, and he will gain knowledge.

Proverbs 22:15

Folly is bound up in the heart of a child, but the rod of discipline will drive it far from him.

Proverbs 23:13, 14

Do not withhold discipline from a child; if you punish him with the rod, he will not die.

Punish him with the rod and save his soul from death.

Proverbs 23:23

Buy the truth and do not sell it; get wisdom, discipline and understanding.

Proverbs 25:12

Like an earring of gold or an ornament of fine gold is a wise man's rebuke to a listening ear.

Proverbs 27:5

Better is open rebuke than hidden love.

Proverbs 28:9

If anyone turns a deaf ear to the law, even his prayers are detestable.

Proverbs 28:14

Blessed is the man who always fears the LORD, but he who hardens his heart falls into trouble.

Proverbs 28:23

He who rebukes a man will in the end gain more favor than he who has a flattering tongue.

Proverbs 29:1

A man who remains stiff-necked after many rebukes will suddenly be destroyed--without remedy.

Proverbs 29:15

The rod of correction imparts wisdom, but a child left to himself disgraces his mother.

Proverbs 29:17

Discipline your son, and he will give you peace; he will bring delight to your soul.

Proverbs 30:5, 6

Every word of God is flawless; he is a shield to those who take refuge in him.

Do not add to his words, or he will rebuke you and prove you a liar.

WISDOM AND UNDERSTANDING

Proverbs 1:1-6

The proverbs of Solomon son of David, king of Israel:

for attaining wisdom and discipline; for understanding words of insight;

for acquiring a disciplined and prudent life, doing what is right and just and fair;

for giving prudence to the simple, knowledge and discretion to the young--

Let the wise listen and add to their learning, and let the discerning get guidance.

for understanding proverbs and parables, the sayings and riddles of the wise.

Proverbs 1:7

The fear of the LORD is the beginning of knowledge, but fools despise wisdom and discipline.

Proverbs 2:1-5

My son, if you accept my words and store up my commands within you, turning your ear to wisdom and applying your heart to understanding,

and if you call out for insight and cry aloud for understanding,

and if you look for it as for silver and search for it as for hidden treasure,

then you will understand the fear of the LORD and find the knowledge of God.

Proverbs 2:6, 7

For the LORD gives wisdom, and from his mouth come knowledge and understanding.

He holds victory in store for the upright, he is a shield to those whose walk is blameless.

Proverbs 2:10-12, 20

For wisdom will enter your heart, and knowledge will be pleasant to your soul.

Discretion will protect you, and understanding will guard you.

Wisdom will save you from the ways of wicked men, from men whose words are perverse,

Thus you will walk in the ways of good men and keep to the paths of the righteous.

Proverbs 3:5

Trust in the LORD with all your heart and lean not on your own understanding;

Proverbs 3:13-18

Blessed is the man who finds wisdom, the man who gains understanding,

for she is more profitable than silver and yields better returns than gold.

She is more precious than rubies; nothing you desire can compare with her.

Long life is in her right hand; in her left hand are riches and honor.

Her ways are pleasant ways, and all her paths are peace.

She is a tree of life to those who embrace her; those who lay hold of her will be blessed.

Proverbs 3:19, 20

By wisdom the LORD laid the earth's foundations, by understanding he set the heavens in place;

By his knowledge the deeps were divided, and the clouds let drop the dew.

Proverbs 3:35

The wise inherit honor, but fools he holds up to shame.

Proverbs 4:1

Listen, my sons, to a father's instruction; pay attention and gain understanding.

Proverbs 4:5-9

Get wisdom, get understanding; do not forget my words or swerve from them.

Do not forsake wisdom, and she will protect you; love her, and she will watch over you.

Wisdom is supreme; therefore get wisdom. Though it cost all you have, get understanding.

Esteem her, and she will exalt you; embrace her, and she will honor you.

She will set a garland of grace on your head and present you with a crown of splendor.

Proverbs 8:5

You who are simple, gain prudence; you who are foolish, gain understanding.

Proverbs 8:10-12, 14

Choose my instruction instead of silver, knowledge rather than choice gold,

for wisdom is more precious than rubies, and nothing you desire can compare with her.

"I, wisdom, dwell together with prudence; I possess knowledge and discretion."

Counsel and sound judgment are mine; I have understanding and power.

Proverbs 8:32-36

"Now then, my sons, listen to me; blessed are those who keep my ways.

Listen to my instruction and be wise; do not ignore it.

Blessed is the man who listens to me, watching daily at my doors, waiting at my doorway.

For whoever finds me finds life and receives favor from the LORD.

But whoever fails to find me harms himself; all who hate me love death."

Proverbs 9:6

Leave your simple ways and you will live; walk in the way of understanding.

Proverbs 9:9

Instruct a wise man and he will be wiser still; teach a righteous man and he will add to his learning.

Proverbs 9:10

The fear of the LORD is the beginning of wisdom, and knowledge of the Holy One is understanding.

Proverbs 9:12

If you are wise, your wisdom will reward you; if you are a mocker, you alone will suffer.

Proverbs 10:1

The proverbs of Solomon: A wise son brings joy to his father, but a foolish son grief to his mother.

Proverbs 10:8

The wise in heart accept commands, but a chattering fool comes to ruin.

Proverbs 10:13

Wisdom is found on the lips of the discerning, but a rod is for the back of him who lacks judgment.

Proverbs 10:14

Wise men store up knowledge, but the mouth of a fool invites ruin.

Proverbs 10:19

When words are many, sin is not absent, but he who holds his tongue is wise.

Proverbs 10:23

A fool finds pleasure in evil conduct, but a man of understanding delights in wisdom.

Proverbs 10:31

The mouth of the righteous brings forth wisdom, but a perverse tongue will be cut out.

Proverbs 11:2

When pride comes, then comes disgrace, but with humility comes wisdom.

Proverbs 11:12

A man who lacks judgment derides his neighbor, but a man of understanding holds his tongue.

Proverbs 12:8

A man is praised according to his wisdom, but men with warped minds are despised.

Proverbs 12:15

The way of a fool seems right to him, but a wise man listens to advice.

Proverbs 12:18

Reckless words pierce like a sword, but the tongue of the wise brings healing.

Proverbs 13:1

A wise son heeds his father's instruction, but a mocker does not listen to rebuke.

Proverbs 13:10

Pride only breeds quarrels, but wisdom is found in those who take advice.

Proverbs 13:14

The teaching of the wise is a fountain of life, turning a man from the snares of death.

Proverbs 13:15

Good understanding wins favor, but the way of the unfaithful is hard.

Proverbs 14:6

The mocker seeks wisdom and finds none, but knowledge comes easily to the discerning.

Proverbs 14:8

The wisdom of the prudent is to give thought to their ways, but the folly of fools is deception.

Proverbs 14:16

A wise man fears the LORD and shuns evil, but a fool is hotheaded and reckless.

Proverbs 14:29

A patient man has great understanding, but a quick-tempered man displays folly.

Proverbs 14:33

Wisdom reposes in the heart of the discerning and even among fools she lets herself be known.

Proverbs 14:35

A king delights in a wise servant, but a shameful servant incurs his wrath.

Proverbs 15:2

The tongue of the wise commends knowledge, but the mouth of the fool gushes folly.

Proverbs 15:7

The lips of the wise spread knowledge; not so the hearts of fools.

Proverbs 15:20

A wise son brings joy to his father, but a foolish man despises his mother.

Proverbs 15:21

Folly delights a man who lacks judgment, but a man of understanding keeps a straight course.

Proverbs 15:24

The path of life leads upward for the wise to keep him from going down to the grave.

Proverbs 15:31

He who listens to a life-giving rebuke will be at home among the wise.

Proverbs 15:32

He who ignores discipline despises himself, but whoever heeds correction gains understanding.

Proverbs 15:33

The fear of the LORD teaches a man wisdom, AND humility comes before honor.

Proverbs 16:16

How much better to get wisdom than gold, to choose understanding rather than silver!

Proverbs 16:21

The wise in heart are called discerning, and pleasant words promote instruction.

Proverbs 16:22

Understanding is a fountain of life to those who have it, but folly brings punishment to fools.

Proverbs 16:23

A wise man's heart guides his mouth, and his lips promote instruction.

Proverbs 17:10

A rebuke impresses a man of discernment more than a hundred lashes a fool.

Proverbs 17:24

A discerning man keeps wisdom in view, but a fool's eyes wander to the ends of the earth.

Proverbs 17:27

A man of knowledge uses words with restraint, and a man of understanding is even-tempered.

Proverbs 18:2

A fool finds no pleasure in understanding but delights in airing his own opinions.

Proverbs 18:4

The words of a man's mouth are deep waters, but the fountain of wisdom is a bubbling brook.

Proverbs 18:15

The heart of the discerning acquires knowledge; the ears of the wise seek it out.

Proverbs 19:8

He who gets wisdom loves his own soul; he who cherishes understanding prospers.

Proverbs 19:11

A man's wisdom gives him patience; it is to his glory to overlook an offense.

Proverbs 19:20

Listen to advice and accept instruction, and in the end you
will be wise.

Proverbs 19:25

Flog a mocker, and the simple will learn prudence; rebuke
a discerning man, and he will gain knowledge.

Proverbs 20:5

The purposes of a man's heart are deep waters, but a man
of understanding draws them out.

Proverbs 21:11

When a mocker is punished, the simple gain wisdom; when
a wise man is instructed, he gets knowledge.

Proverbs 21:16

A man who strays from the path of understanding comes to
rest in the company of the dead.

Proverbs 21:20

In the house of the wise are stores of choice food and oil,
but a foolish man devours all he has.

Proverbs 21:22

A wise man attacks the city of the mighty and pulls down the stronghold in which they trust.

Proverbs 21:30

There is no wisdom, no insight, no plan that can succeed against the LORD.

Proverbs 23:4

Do not wear yourself out to get rich; have the wisdom to show restraint.

Proverbs 23:15, 16

My son, if your heart is wise, then my heart will be glad;

my inmost being will rejoice when your lips speak what is right.

Proverbs 23:19

Listen, my son, and be wise, and keep your heart on the right path.

Proverbs 23:23

Buy the truth and do not sell it; get wisdom, discipline and understanding.

Proverbs 24:3, 4

By wisdom a house is built, and through understanding it is established;

through knowledge its rooms are filled with rare and beautiful treasures.

Proverbs 24:5

A wise man has great power, and a man of knowledge increases strength.

Proverbs 24:13, 14

Eat honey, my son, for it is good; honey from the comb is sweet to your taste.

Know also that wisdom is sweet to your soul; if you find it, there is a future hope for you, and your hope will not be cut off.

Proverbs 24:23

These also are sayings of the wise: To show partiality in judging is not good.

Proverbs 28:2

When a country is rebellious, it has many rulers, but a man of understanding and knowledge maintains order.

Proverbs 28:5

Evil men do not understand justice, but those who seek the LORD understand it fully.

Proverbs 28:11

A rich man may be wise in his own eyes, but a poor man who has discernment sees through him.

Proverbs 28:16

A tyrannical ruler lacks judgment, but he who hates ill-gotten gain will enjoy a long life.

Proverbs 28:26

He who trusts in himself is a fool, but he who walks in wisdom is kept safe.

Proverbs 29:3

A man who loves wisdom brings joy to his father, but a companion of prostitutes squanders his wealth.

Proverbs 29:8

Mockers stir up a city, but wise men turn away anger.

Proverbs 29:9

If a wise man goes to court with a fool, the fool rages and scoffs, and there is no peace

Proverbs 29:11

A fool gives full vent to his anger, but a wise man keeps himself under control.

Proverbs 29:15

The rod of correction imparts wisdom, but a child left to himself disgraces his mother.

Proverbs 30:24-28

Four things on earth are small, yet they are extremely wise:

Ants are creatures of little strength, yet they store up their food in the summer;

coneys are creatures of little power, yet they make their home in the crags;

locusts have no king, yet they advance together in ranks;

a lizard can be caught with the hand, yet it is found in kings' palaces.

PART THREE

Self-Control

ANGER

Proverbs 14:17

A quick-tempered man does foolish things, and a crafty man is hated.

Proverbs 14:29

A patient man has great understanding, but a quick-tempered man displays folly.

Proverbs 15:1

A gentle answer turns away wrath, but a harsh word stirs up anger.

Proverbs 15:18

A hot-tempered man stirs up dissension, but a patient man calms a quarrel.

Proverbs 16:14

A king's wrath is a messenger of death, but a wise man will appease it.

Proverbs 16:32

Better a patient man than a warrior, a man who controls his temper than one who takes a city.

Proverbs 19:11

A man's wisdom gives him patience; it is to his glory to overlook an offense.

Proverbs 19:19

A hot-tempered man must pay the penalty; if you rescue him, you will have to do it again.

Proverbs 20:2

A king's wrath is like the roar of a lion; he who angers him forfeits his life.

Proverbs 21:14

A gift given in secret soothes anger, and a bribe concealed in the cloak pacifies great wrath.

Proverbs 21:19

Better to live in a desert than with a quarrelsome and ill-tempered wife.

Proverbs 21:24

The proud and arrogant man--"Mocker" is his name; he behaves with overweening pride.

Proverbs 22:24

Do not make friends with a hot-tempered man, do not associate with one easily angered.

Proverbs 27:3

Stone is heavy and sand a burden, but provocation by a fool is heavier than both.

Proverbs 27:4

Anger is cruel and fury overwhelming, but who can stand before jealousy?

Proverbs 29:8

Mockers stir up a city, but wise men turn away anger.

Proverbs 29:22

An angry man stirs up dissension, and a hot-tempered one commits many sins.

Proverbs 30:33

For as churning the milk produces butter, and as twisting the nose produces blood, so stirring up anger produces strife.

DILIGENCE

Proverbs 4:23

Above all else, guard your heart, for it is the wellspring of
life.

Proverbs 10:4

Lazy hands make a man poor, but diligent hands bring
wealth.

Proverbs 12:24

Diligent hands will rule, but laziness ends in slave labor.

Proverbs 12:27

The lazy man does not roast his game, but the diligent man
prizes his possessions.

Proverbs 13:4

The sluggard craves and gets nothing, but the desires of the
diligent are fully satisfied.

Proverbs 21:5

The plans of the diligent lead to profit as surely as haste leads to poverty.

Proverbs 22:29

Do you see a man skilled in his work? He will serve before kings; he will not serve before obscure men.

Proverbs 27:23, 27

Be sure you know the condition of your flocks, give careful attention to your herds;

You will have plenty of goats' milk to feed you and your family and to nourish your servant girls.

DRINKING

Proverbs 20:1

Wine is a mocker and beer a brawler; whoever is led astray by them is not wise.

Proverbs 21:17

He who loves pleasure will become poor; whoever loves wine and oil will never be rich.

Proverbs 23:20, 21

Do not join those who drink too much wine or gorge themselves on meat,

for drunkards and gluttons become poor, and drowsiness clothes them in rags.

Proverbs 23:29-35

Who has woe? Who has sorrow? Who has strife? Who has complaints? Who has needless bruises? Who has bloodshot eyes?

Those who linger over wine, who go to sample bowls of mixed wine.

Do not gaze at wine when it is red, when it sparkles in the cup, when it goes down smoothly!

In the end it bites like a snake and poisons like a viper.

Your eyes will see strange sights and your mind imagine confusing things.

You will be like one sleeping on the high seas, lying on top of the rigging.

"They hit me," you will say, "but I'm not hurt! They beat me, but I don't feel it! When will I wake up so I can find another drink?"

Proverbs 31:4-7

It is not for kings, O Lemuel--not for kings to drink wine, not for rulers to crave beer,

lest they drink and forget what the law decrees, and deprive all the oppressed of their rights.

Give beer to those who are perishing, wine to those who are in anguish;

let them drink and forget their poverty and remember their misery no more.

ENVY AND JEALOUSY

Proverbs 6:34, 35

For jealousy arouses a husband's fury, and he will show no mercy when he takes revenge.

He will not accept any compensation; he will refuse the bribe, however great it is.

Proverbs 14:30

A heart at peace gives life to the body, but envy rots the bones.

Proverbs 27:4

Anger is cruel and fury overwhelming, but who can stand before jealousy?

ENVY OF EVILDOERS

Proverbs 1:31-33

They will eat the fruit of their ways and be filled with the fruit of their schemes.

For the waywardness of the simple will kill them, and the complacency of fools will destroy them;

but whoever listens to me will live in safety and be at ease, without fear of harm.

Proverbs 2:21, 22

For the upright will live in the land, and the blameless will remain in it;

but the wicked will be cut off from the land, and the unfaithful will be torn from it.

Proverbs 3:31, 32

Do not envy a violent man or choose any of his ways,

for the LORD detests a perverse man but takes the upright into his confidence.

Proverbs 8:13

To fear the LORD is to hate evil; I hate pride and arrogance, evil behavior and perverse speech.

Proverbs 10:3

The LORD does not let the righteous go hungry but he thwarts the craving of the wicked.

Proverbs 10:25

When the storm has swept by, the wicked are gone, but the righteous stand firm forever.

Proverbs 10:27-30

The fear of the LORD adds length to life, but the years of the wicked are cut short.

The prospect of the righteous is joy, but the hopes of the wicked come to nothing.

The way of the LORD is a refuge for the righteous, but it is the ruin of those who do evil.

The righteous will never be uprooted, but the wicked will not remain in the land.

Proverbs 11:3

The integrity of the upright guides them, but the unfaithful are destroyed by their duplicity.

Proverbs 11:5, 6

The righteousness of the blameless makes a straight way for them, but the wicked are brought down by their own wickedness.

The righteousness of the upright delivers them, but the unfaithful are trapped by evil desires.

Proverbs 11:21

Be sure of this: The wicked will not go unpunished, but those who are righteous will go free.

Proverbs 11:31

If the righteous receive their due on earth, how much more the ungodly and the sinner!

Proverbs 12:7

Wicked men are overthrown and are no more, but the house of the righteous stands firm.

Proverbs 13:9

The light of the righteous shines brightly, but the lamp of the wicked is snuffed out.

Proverbs 22:12

The eyes of the LORD keep watch over knowledge, but he frustrates the words of the unfaithful.

Proverbs 23:6

Do not eat the food of a stingy man, do not crave his delicacies.

Proverbs 23:17, 18

Do not let your heart envy sinners, but always be zealous for the fear of the LORD.

There is surely a future hope for you, and your hope will not be cut off.

Proverbs 24:1, 2

Do not envy wicked men, do not desire their company;

for their hearts plot violence, and their lips talk about making trouble.

Proverbs 24:19, 20

Do not fret because of evil men or be envious of the wicked,

for the evil man has no future hope, and the lamp of the wicked will be snuffed out.

FEAR

Proverbs 1:33

But whoever listens to me will live in safety and be at ease, without fear of harm.

Proverbs 3:21, 24

My son, preserve sound judgment and discernment, do not let them out of your sight;

when you lie down, you will not be afraid; when you lie down, your sleep will be sweet.

Proverbs 3:25, 26

Have no fear of sudden disaster or of the ruin that overtakes the wicked,

for the LORD will be your confidence and will keep your foot from being snared.

Proverbs 10:24

What the wicked dreads will overtake him; what the righteous desire will be granted.

Proverbs 29:25

Fear of man will prove to be a snare, but whoever trusts in the LORD is kept safe.

GREED AND COVETOUSNESS

Proverbs 1:18, 19

These men lie in wait for their own blood; they waylay only themselves!

Such is the end of all who go after ill-gotten gain; it takes away the lives of those who get it.

Proverbs 13:25

The righteous eat to their hearts' content, but the stomach of the wicked goes hungry.

Proverbs 15:16

Better a little with the fear of the LORD than great wealth with turmoil.

Proverbs 15:27

A greedy man brings trouble to his family, but he who hates bribes will live.

Proverbs 22:1

A good name is more desirable than great riches; to be esteemed is better than silver or gold.

Proverbs 22:4

Humility and the fear of the LORD bring wealth and honor and life.

Proverbs 25:16

If you find honey, eat just enough--too much of it, and you will vomit.

Proverbs 27:20

Death and Destruction are never satisfied, and neither are the eyes of man.

Proverbs 28:6

Better a poor man whose walk is blameless than a rich man whose ways are perverse.

Proverbs 28:8

He who increases his wealth by exorbitant interest amasses it for another, who will be kind to the poor.

Proverbs 28:16

A tyrannical ruler lacks judgment, but he who hates ill-gotten gain will enjoy a long life.

Proverbs 28:25

A greedy man stirs up dissension, but he who trusts in the LORD will prosper.

Proverbs 29:4

By justice a king gives a country stability, but one who is greedy for bribes tears it down.

HASTE

Proverbs 4:26

Make level paths for your feet and take only ways that are firm.

Proverbs 14:29

A patient man has great understanding, but a quick-tempered man displays folly.

Proverbs 18:13

He who answers before listening--that is his folly and his shame.

Proverbs 19:2

It is not good to have zeal without knowledge, nor to be hasty and miss the way.

Proverbs 20:21

An inheritance quickly gained at the beginning will not be blessed at the end.

Proverbs 21:5

The plans of the diligent lead to profit as surely as haste leads to poverty.

Proverbs 25:8

Do not bring hastily to court, for what will you do in the end if your neighbor puts you to shame?

Proverbs 28:20

A faithful man will be richly blessed, but one eager to get rich will not go unpunished.

Proverbs 28:22

A stingy man is eager to get rich and is unaware that poverty awaits him.

Proverbs 29:20

Do you see a man who speaks in haste? There is more hope for a fool than for him.

HATE

Proverbs 8:13

To fear the LORD is to hate evil; I hate pride and arrogance, evil behavior and perverse speech.

Proverbs 10:12

Hatred stirs up dissension, but love covers over all wrongs.

Proverbs 10:18

He who conceals his hatred has lying lips, and whoever spreads slander is a fool.

Proverbs 11:12

A man who lacks judgment derides his neighbor, but a man of understanding holds his tongue.

Proverbs 12:1

Whoever loves discipline loves knowledge, but he who hates correction is stupid.

Proverbs 13:5

The righteous hate what is false, but the wicked bring shame and disgrace.

Proverbs 14:21

He who despises his neighbor sins, but blessed is he who is kind to the needy.

Proverbs 15:10

Stern discipline awaits him who leaves the path; he who hates correction will die.

Proverbs 15:17

Better a meal of vegetables where there is love than a fattened calf with hatred.

Proverbs 26:24

A malicious man disguises himself with his lips, but in his heart he harbors deceit.

Proverbs 26:26

His malice may be concealed by deception, but his wickedness will be exposed in the assembly.

Proverbs 26:28

A lying tongue hates those it hurts, and a flattering mouth works ruin.

JUMPING TO CONCLUSIONS

Proverbs 18:13

He who answers before listening--that is his folly and his shame.

Proverbs 25:8

Do not bring hastily to court, for what will you do in the end if your neighbor puts you to shame?

Proverbs 29:20

Do you see a man who speaks in haste? There is more hope for a fool than for him.

PRIDE

Proverbs 6:16, 17

There are six things the LORD hates, seven that are detestable to him:

haughty eyes, a lying tongue, hands that shed innocent blood.

Proverbs 8:13

To fear the LORD is to hate evil; I hate pride and arrogance, evil behavior and perverse speech.

Proverbs 11:2

When pride comes, then comes disgrace, but with humility comes wisdom.

Proverbs 13:10

Pride only breeds quarrels, but wisdom is found in those who take advice.

Proverbs 15:25

The LORD tears down the proud man's house but he keeps the widow's boundaries intact.

Proverbs 16:5

The LORD detests all the proud of heart. Be sure of this: They will not go unpunished.

Proverbs 16:18

Pride goes before destruction, a haughty spirit before a fall.

Proverbs 16:19

Better to be lowly in spirit and among the oppressed than to share plunder with the proud.

Proverbs 18:12

Before his downfall a man's heart is proud, but humility comes before honor.

Proverbs 21:4

Haughty eyes and a proud heart, the lamp of the wicked, are sin!

Proverbs 21:24

The proud and arrogant man--"Mocker" is his name; he behaves with overweening pride.

Proverbs 25:6, 7a

Do not exalt yourself in the king's presence, and do not claim a place among great men;

it is better for him to say to you, "Come up here," than for him to humiliate you before a nobleman.

Proverbs 25:27

It is not good to eat too much honey, nor is it honorable to seek one's own honor.

Proverbs 26:12

Do you see a man wise in his own eyes? There is more hope for a fool than for him.

Proverbs 29:23

A man's pride brings him low, but a man of lowly spirit gains honor.

Proverbs 30:32

If you have played the fool and exalted yourself, or if you have planned evil, clap your hand over your mouth!

SELFISHNESS

Proverbs 3:27, 28

Do not withhold good from those who deserve it, when it is in your power to act.

Do not say to your neighbor, "Come back later; I'll give it tomorrow"--when you now have it with you.

Proverbs 13:7

One man pretends to be rich, yet has nothing; another pretends to be poor, yet has great wealth.

Proverbs 18:1

An unfriendly man pursues selfish ends; he defies all sound judgment.

Proverbs 19:17

He who is kind to the poor lends to the LORD, and he will reward him for what he has done.

Proverbs 21:25, 26

The sluggard's craving will be the death of him, because his hands refuse to work.

All day long he craves for more, but the righteous give
without sparing.

Proverbs 22:9

A generous man will himself be blessed, for he shares his
food with the poor.

Proverbs 23:6

Do not eat the food of a stingy man, do not crave his
delicacies;

Proverbs 24:11, 12

Rescue those being led away to death; hold back those
staggering toward slaughter.

If you say, "But we knew nothing about this," does not he
who weighs the heart perceive it? Does not he who guards
your life know it? Will he not repay each person according
to what he has done?

Proverbs 28:22

A stingy man is eager to get rich and is unaware that
poverty awaits him.

Proverbs 28:27

He who gives to the poor will lack nothing, but he who
closes his eyes to them receives many curses.

SELF-CONTROL

Proverbs 14:29

A patient man has great understanding, but a quick-tempered man displays folly.

Proverbs 15:18

A hot-tempered man stirs up dissension, but a patient man calms a quarrel.

Proverbs 16:32

Better a patient man than a warrior, a man who controls his temper than one who takes a city.

Proverbs 19:11

A man's wisdom gives him patience; it is to his glory to overlook an offense.

Proverbs 21:17

He who loves pleasure will become poor; whoever loves wine and oil will never be rich.

Proverbs 23:1-3

When you sit to dine with a ruler, note well what is before you,

and put a knife to your throat if you are given to gluttony.

Do not crave his delicacies, for that food is deceptive.

Proverbs 25:15

Through patience a ruler can be persuaded, and a gentle tongue can break a bone.

Proverbs 25:16

If you find honey, eat just enough-- too much of it, and you will vomit.

Proverbs 25:27

It is not good to eat too much honey, nor is it honorable to seek one's own honor.

Proverbs 25:28

Like a city whose walls are broken down is a man who lacks self-control.

SELF-SATISFACTION

Proverbs 12:14

From the fruit of his lips a man is filled with good things as surely as the work of his hands rewards him.

Proverbs 13:19

A longing fulfilled is sweet to the soul, but fools detest turning from evil.

Proverbs 14:14

The faithless will be fully repaid for their ways, and the good man rewarded for his.

Proverbs 16:20

Whoever gives heed to instruction prospers, and blessed is he who trusts in the LORD.

Proverbs 21:2

All a man's ways seem right to him, but the LORD weighs the heart.

SLEEPING AND RISING

Proverbs 3:21, 24

My son, preserve sound judgment and discernment, do not let them out of your sight;

when you lie down, you will not be afraid; when you lie down, your sleep will be sweet.

Proverbs 6:9-11; 24:33, 34

How long will you lie there, you sluggard? When will you get up from your sleep?

A little sleep, a little slumber, a little folding of the hands to rest--

and poverty will come on you like a bandit and scarcity like an armed man.

Proverbs 6:20, 22

My son, keep your father's commands and do not forsake your mother's teaching.

When you walk, they will guide you; when you sleep, they will watch over you; when you awake, they will speak to you.

133

Proverbs 10:5

He who gathers crops in summer is a wise son, but he who sleeps during harvest is a disgraceful son.

Proverbs 19:15

Laziness brings on deep sleep, and the shiftless man goes hungry.

Proverbs 20:13

Do not love sleep or you will grow poor; stay awake and you will have food to spare.

Proverbs 26:14

As a door turns on its hinges, so a sluggard turns on his bed.

TEMPER

Proverbs 14:29

A patient man has great understanding, but a quick-tempered man displays folly.

Proverbs 16:32

Better a patient man than a warrior, a man who controls his temper than one who takes a city.

Proverbs 17:27

A man of knowledge uses words with restraint, and a man of understanding is even-tempered.

Proverbs 19:11

A man's wisdom gives him patience; it is to his glory to overlook an offense.

Proverbs 25:28

Like a city whose walls are broken down is a man who lacks self-control.

TEMPTATION

Proverbs 1:10, 15

My son, if sinners entice you, do not give in to them.

My son, do not go along with them, do not set foot on their paths.

Proverbs 3:5, 6

Trust in the LORD with all your heart and lean not on your own understanding;

in all your ways acknowledge him, and he will make your paths straight.

Proverbs 3:7, 8

Do not be wise in your own eyes; fear the LORD and shun evil.

This will bring health to your body and nourishment to your bones.

Proverbs 4:25-27

Let your eyes look straight ahead, fix your gaze directly before you.

Make level paths for your feet and take only ways that are firm.

Do not swerve to the right or the left; keep your foot from evil.

Proverbs 8:13

To fear the LORD is to hate evil; I hate pride and arrogance, evil behavior and perverse speech.

Proverbs 10:2

Ill-gotten treasures are of no value, but righteousness delivers from death.

Proverbs 10:9

The man of integrity walks securely, but he who takes crooked paths will be found out.

Proverbs 11:5, 6

The righteousness of the blameless makes a straight way for them, but the wicked are brought down by their own wickedness.

The righteousness of the upright delivers them, but the unfaithful are trapped by evil desires.

Proverbs 11:8

The righteous man is rescued from trouble, and it comes on the wicked instead.

Proverbs 12:3

A man cannot be established through wickedness, but the righteous cannot be uprooted.

Proverbs 12:13

An evil man is trapped by his sinful talk, but a righteous man escapes trouble.

Proverbs 14:12

There is a way that seems right to a man, but in the end it leads to death.

Proverbs 14:16

A wise man fears the LORD and shuns evil, but a fool is hotheaded and reckless.

Proverbs 14:22

Do not those who plot evil go astray? But those who plan what is good find love and faithfulness.

Proverbs 15:3

The eyes of the LORD are everywhere, keeping watch on the wicked and the good.

Proverbs 15:9

The LORD detests the way of the wicked but he loves those who pursue righteousness.

Proverbs 16:6

Through love and faithfulness sin is atoned for; through the fear of the LORD a man avoids evil.

Proverbs 16:8

Better a little with righteousness than much gain with injustice.

Proverbs 16:17

The highway of the upright avoids evil; he who guards his way guards his life.

Proverbs 16:19

Better to be lowly in spirit and among the oppressed than to share plunder with the proud.

Proverbs 19:1

Better a poor man whose walk is blameless than a fool whose lips are perverse.

Proverbs 19:21

Many are the plans in a man's heart, but it is the LORD'S purpose that prevails.

Proverbs 20:17

Food gained by fraud tastes sweet to a man, but he ends up with a mouth full of gravel.

Proverbs 21:15

When justice is done, it brings joy to the righteous but terror to evildoers.

Proverbs 28:6

Better a poor man whose walk is blameless than a rich man whose ways are perverse.

Proverbs 28:26

He who trusts in himself is a fool, but he who walks in wisdom is kept safe.

Proverbs 29:6

An evil man is snared by his own sin, but a righteous one can sing and be glad.

PART FOUR

Control
of Mouth

ARGUING AND STRIFE

Proverbs 3:30

Do not accuse a man for no reason--when he has done you no harm.

Proverbs 6:12, 14

A scoundrel and villain, who goes about with a corrupt mouth,

who plots evil with deceit in his heart--he always stirs up dissension.

Proverbs 6:16, 19

There are six things the LORD hates, seven that are detestable to him:

a false witness who pours out lies and a man who stirs up dissension among brothers.

Proverbs 10:12

Hatred stirs up dissension, but love covers over all wrongs.

Proverbs 13:10

Pride only breeds quarrels, but wisdom is found in those who take advice.

Proverbs 15:18

A hot-tempered man stirs up dissension, but a patient man calms a quarrel.

Proverbs 16:28

A perverse man stirs up dissension, and a gossip separates close friends.

Proverbs 17:1

Better a dry crust with peace and quiet than a house full of feasting, with strife.

Proverbs 17:14

Starting a quarrel is like breaching a dam; so drop the matter before a dispute breaks out.

Proverbs 17:19

He who loves a quarrel loves sin; he who builds a high gate invites destruction.

Proverbs 18:6

A fool's lips bring him strife, and his mouth invites a beating.

Proverbs 18:19

An offended brother is more unyielding than a fortified city, and disputes are like the barred gates of a citadel.

Proverbs 20:3

It is to a man's honor to avoid strife, but every fool is quick to quarrel.

Proverbs 22:10

Drive out the mocker, and out goes strife; quarrels and insults are ended.

Proverbs 23:29, 30

Who has woe? Who has sorrow? Who has strife? Who has complaints? Who has needless bruises? Who has bloodshot eyes?

Those who linger over wine, who go to sample bowls of mixed wine.

Proverbs 25:8

Do not bring hastily to court, for what will you do in the end if your neighbor puts you to shame?

Proverbs 25:24

Better to live on a corner of the roof than share a house with a quarrelsome wife.

Proverbs 26:17

Like one who seizes a dog by the ears is a passer-by who meddles in a quarrel not his own.

Proverbs 26:20

Without wood a fire goes out; without gossip a quarrel
dies down.

Proverbs 26:21

As charcoal to embers and as wood to fire, so is a quarrelsome man for kindling strife.

Proverbs 27:15

A quarrelsome wife is like a constant dripping on a rainy day.

Proverbs 28:25

A greedy man stirs up dissension, but he who trusts in the
LORD will prosper.

Proverbs 29:9

If a wise man goes to court with a fool, the fool rages and
scoffs, and there is no peace.

Proverbs 29:22

An angry man stirs up dissension, and a hot-tempered one
commits many sins.

Proverbs 30:33

For as churning the milk produces butter, and as twisting the
nose produces blood, so stirring up anger produces strife.

BOASTING

Proverbs 25:14

Like clouds and wind without rain is a man who boasts of gifts he does not give.

Proverbs 25:27

It is not good to eat too much honey, nor is it honorable to seek one's own honor.

Proverbs 27:1

Do not boast about tomorrow, for you do not know what a day may bring forth.

Proverbs 27:2

Let another praise you, and not your own mouth; someone else, and not your own lips.

COMPLAINING

Proverbs 15:4

The tongue that brings healing is a tree of life, but a deceitful tongue crushes the spirit.

Proverbs 15:15

All the days of the oppressed are wretched, but the cheerful heart has a continual feast.

Proverbs 17:22

A cheerful heart is good medicine, but a crushed spirit dries up the bones.

Proverbs 21:19

Better to live in a desert than with a quarrelsome and ill-tempered wife.

Proverbs 25:24

Better to live on a corner of the roof than share a house with a quarrelsome wife.

Proverbs 27:15

A quarrelsome wife is like a constant dripping on a rainy day.

CONTROL OF MOUTH

Proverbs 4:24

Put away perversity from your mouth; keep corrupt talk far from your lips.

Proverbs 6:1, 2

My son, if you have put up security for your neighbor, if you have struck hands in pledge for another,

if you have been trapped by what you said, ensnared by the words of your mouth.

Proverbs 8:13

To fear the LORD is to hate evil; I hate pride and arrogance, evil behavior and perverse speech.

Proverbs 10:11

The mouth of the righteous is a fountain of life, but violence overwhelms the mouth of the wicked.

Proverbs 10:14

Wise men store up knowledge, but the mouth of a fool invites ruin.

Proverbs 10:19

When words are many, sin is not absent, but he who holds his tongue is wise.

Proverbs 10:20, 21

The tongue of the righteous is choice silver, but the heart of the wicked is of little value.

The lips of the righteous nourish many, but fools die for lack of judgment.

Proverbs 10:31, 32

The mouth of the righteous brings forth wisdom, but a perverse tongue will be cut out.

The lips of the righteous know what is fitting, but the mouth of the wicked only what is perverse.

Proverbs 11:9

With his mouth the godless destroys his neighbor, but through knowledge the righteous escape.

Proverbs 11:11

Through the blessing of the upright a city is exalted, but by the mouth of the wicked it is destroyed.

Proverbs 12:13

An evil man is trapped by his sinful talk, but a righteous man escapes trouble.

Proverbs 12:14

From the fruit of his lips a man is filled with good things as surely as the work of his hands rewards him.

Proverbs 12:18

Reckless words pierce like a sword, but the tongue of the wise brings healing.

Proverbs 13:2

From the fruit of his lips a man enjoys good things, but the unfaithful have a craving for violence.

Proverbs 13:3

He who guards his lips guards his life, but he who speaks rashly will come to ruin.

Proverbs 14:3

A fool's talk brings a rod to his back, but the lips of the wise protect them.

Proverbs 14:23

All hard work brings a profit, but mere talk leads only to poverty.

Proverbs 15:1

A gentle answer turns away wrath, but a harsh word stirs up anger.

Proverbs 15:2

The tongue of the wise commends knowledge, but the mouth of the fool gushes folly.

Proverbs 15:4

The tongue that brings healing is a tree of life, but a deceitful tongue crushes the spirit.

Proverbs 15:7

The lips of the wise spread knowledge; not so the hearts of fools.

Proverbs 15:23

A man finds joy in giving an apt reply--and how good is a timely word!

Proverbs 15:14

The discerning heart seeks knowledge, but the mouth of a fool feeds on folly.

Proverbs 15:26

The LORD detests the thoughts of the wicked, but those of the pure are pleasing to him.

Proverbs 15:28

The heart of the righteous weighs its answers, but the mouth of the wicked gushes evil.

Proverbs 16:1

To man belong the plans of the heart, but from the LORD comes the reply of the tongue.

Proverbs 16:10

The lips of a king speak as an oracle, and his mouth should not betray justice.

Proverbs 16:13

Kings take pleasure in honest lips; they value a man who speaks the truth.

Proverbs 16:21

The wise in heart are called discerning, and pleasant words promote instruction.

Proverbs 16:23

A wise man's heart guides his mouth, and his lips promote instruction.

Proverbs 16:24

Pleasant words are a honeycomb, sweet to the soul and healing to the bones.

Proverbs 16:27

A scoundrel plots evil, and his speech is like a scorching fire.

Proverbs 17:7

Arrogant lips are unsuited to a fool-- how much worse lying lips to a ruler!

Proverbs 17:20

A man of perverse heart does not prosper; he whose tongue is deceitful falls into trouble.

Proverbs 17:27

A man of knowledge uses words with restraint, and a man of understanding is even-tempered.

Proverbs 17:28

Even a fool is thought wise if he keeps silent, and discerning if he holds his tongue.

Proverbs 18:6

A fool's lips bring him strife, and his mouth invites a beating.

Proverbs 18:7

A fool's mouth is his undoing, and his lips are a snare to his soul.

Proverbs 18:20

From the fruit of his mouth a man's stomach is filled; with the harvest from his lips he is satisfied.

Proverbs 18:21

The tongue has the power of life and death, and those who love it will eat its fruit.

Proverbs 19:1

Better a poor man whose walk is blameless than a fool whose lips are perverse.

Proverbs 20:15

Gold there is, and rubies in abundance, but lips that speak knowledge are a rare jewel.

Proverbs 21:9; 25:24

Better to live on a corner of the roof than share a house with a quarrelsome wife.

Proverbs 21:23

He who guards his mouth and his tongue keeps himself from calamity.

Proverbs 23:9

Do not speak to a fool, for he will scorn the wisdom of your words.

Proverbs 24:26

An honest answer is like a kiss on the lips.

Proverbs 25:11

A word aptly spoken is like apples of gold in settings of silver.

Proverbs 25:23

As a north wind brings rain, so a sly tongue brings angry looks.

Proverbs 26:22

The words of a gossip are like choice morsels; they go down to a man's inmost parts.

Proverbs 26:23

Like a coating of glaze over earthenware are fervent lips with an evil heart.

Proverbs 26:28

A lying tongue hates those it hurts, and a flattering mouth works ruin.

Proverbs 27:15

A quarrelsome wife is like a constant dripping on a rainy day.

Proverbs 29:11

A fool gives full vent to his anger, but a wise man keeps himself under control.

Proverbs 29:20

Do you see a man who speaks in haste? There is more hope for a fool than for him.

EVIL SPEAKING

Proverbs 2:11-14

Discretion will protect you, and understanding will guard you.

Wisdom will save you from the ways of wicked men, from men whose words are perverse,

who leave the straight paths to walk in dark ways,

who delight in doing wrong and rejoice in the perverseness of evil.

Proverbs 4:24

Put away perversity from your mouth; keep corrupt talk far from your lips.

Proverbs 6:12, 14

A scoundrel and villain, who goes about with a corrupt mouth,

who plots evil with deceit in his heart--he always stirs up dissension.

Proverbs 8:13

To fear the LORD is to hate evil; I hate pride and arrogance, evil behavior and perverse speech.

Proverbs 10:18

He who conceals his hatred has lying lips, and whoever spreads slander is a fool.

Proverbs 10:31

The mouth of the righteous brings forth wisdom, but a perverse tongue will be cut out.

Proverbs 10:32

The lips of the righteous know what is fitting, but the mouth of the wicked only what is perverse.

Proverbs 12:13

An evil man is trapped by his sinful talk, but a righteous man escapes trouble.

Proverbs 19:1

Better a poor man whose walk is blameless than a fool whose lips are perverse.

Proverbs 30:32

If you have played the fool and exalted yourself, or if you have planned evil, clap your hand over your mouth!

FLATTERY

Proverbs 20:19

A gossip betrays a confidence; so avoid a man who talks too much.

Proverbs 26:28

A lying tongue hates those it hurts, and a flattering mouth works ruin.

Proverbs 28:23

He who rebukes a man will in the end gain more favor than he who has a flattering tongue.

Proverbs 29:5

Whoever flatters his neighbor is spreading a net for his feet.

GOSSIP

Proverbs 6:16, 19

There are six things the LORD hates, seven that are detestable to him:

a false witness who pours out lies and a man who stirs up dissension among brothers.

Proverbs 10:12

Hatred stirs up dissension, but love covers over all wrongs.

Proverbs 11:9

With his mouth the godless destroys his neighbor, but through knowledge the righteous escape.

Proverbs 11:12

A man who lacks judgment derides his neighbor, but a man of understanding holds his tongue.

Proverbs 11:13

A gossip betrays a confidence, but a trustworthy man keeps a secret.

Proverbs 16:27

A scoundrel plots evil, and his speech is like a scorching fire.

Proverbs 16:28

A perverse man stirs up dissension, and a gossip separates close friends.

Proverbs 17:9

He who covers over an offense promotes love, but whoever repeats the matter separates close friends.

Proverbs 18:8; 26:22

The words of a gossip are like choice morsels; they go down to a man's inmost parts.

Proverbs 20:19

A gossip betrays a confidence; so avoid a man who talks too much.

Proverbs 25:9, 10

If you argue your case with a neighbor, do not betray another man's confidence,

or he who hears it may shame you and you will never lose your bad reputation.

Proverbs 26:20

Without wood a fire goes out; without gossip a quarrel dies down.

Proverbs 26:22

The words of a gossip are like choice morsels; they go down to a man's inmost parts.

LYING

Proverbs 6:16, 17, 19

There are six things the LORD hates, seven that are detestable to him:

haughty eyes, a lying tongue, hands that shed innocent blood,

a false witness who pours out lies and a man who stirs up dissension among brothers.

Proverbs 10:18

He who conceals his hatred has lying lips, and whoever spreads slander is a fool.

Proverbs 14:5

A truthful witness does not deceive, but a false witness pours out lies.

Proverbs 12:17

A truthful witness gives honest testimony, but a false witness tells lies.

Proverbs 12:19

Truthful lips endure forever, but a lying tongue lasts only a moment.

Proverbs 12:20

There is deceit in the hearts of those who plot evil, but joy for those who promote peace.

Proverbs 12:22

The LORD detests lying lips, but he delights in men who are truthful.

Proverbs 13:5

The righteous hate what is false, but the wicked bring shame and disgrace.

Proverbs 14:5

A truthful witness does not deceive, but a false witness pours out lies.

Proverbs 14:25

A truthful witness saves lives, but a false witness is deceitful.

Proverbs 17:4

A wicked man listens to evil lips; a liar pays attention to a malicious tongue.

Proverbs 17:7

Arrogant lips are unsuited to a fool-- how much worse lying lips to a ruler!

Proverbs 19:5

A false witness will not go unpunished, and he who pours out lies will not go free.

Proverbs 19:9

A false witness will not go unpunished, and he who pours out lies will perish.

Proverbs 19:22

What a man desires is unfailing love; better to be poor than a liar.

Proverbs 20:17

Food gained by fraud tastes sweet to a man, but he ends up with a mouth full of gravel.

Proverbs 21:6

A fortune made by a lying tongue is a fleeting vapor and a deadly snare.

Proverbs 21:28

A false witness will perish, and whoever listens to him will be destroyed forever.

Proverbs 24:28, 29

Do not testify against your neighbor without cause, or use your lips to deceive.

Do not say, "I'll do to him as he has done to me; I'll pay that man back for what he did."

Proverbs 25:14

Like clouds and wind without rain is a man who boasts of gifts he does not give.

Proverbs 25:18

Like a club or a sword or a sharp arrow is the man who gives false testimony against his neighbor.

Proverbs 26:18, 19

Like a madman shooting firebrands or deadly arrows

is a man who deceives his neighbor and says, "I was only joking!"

Proverbs 26:28

A lying tongue hates those it hurts, and a flattering mouth works ruin.

Proverbs 28:13

He who conceals his sins does not prosper, but whoever confesses and renounces them finds mercy.

Proverbs 30:5, 6

Every word of God is flawless; he is a shield to those who take refuge in him.

Do not add to his words, or he will rebuke you and prove you a liar.

Proverbs 30:8

Keep falsehood and lies far from me; give me neither poverty nor riches, but give me only my daily bread.

TATTLETALES

Proverbs 10:12

Hatred stirs up dissension, but love covers over all wrongs.

Proverbs 17:9

He who covers over an offense promotes love, but whoever repeats the matter separates close friends.

Proverbs 19:11

A man's wisdom gives him patience; it is to his glory to overlook an offense.

Proverbs 25:9, 10

If you argue your case with a neighbor, do not betray another man's confidence,

or he who hears it may shame you and you will never lose your bad reputation.

TEASING

Proverbs 3:30

Do not accuse a man for no reason--when he has done you no harm.

Proverbs 10:23

A fool finds pleasure in evil conduct, but a man of under-standing delights in wisdom.

Proverbs 26:18, 19

Like a madman shooting firebrands or deadly arrows

is a man who deceives his neighbor and says, "I was only joking!"

PART FIVE

Relationships

AVOIDING BAD ASSOCIATIONS

Proverbs 1:10, 15

My son, if sinners entice you, do not give in to them.

my son, do not go along with them, do not set foot on their paths.

Proverbs 2:10-12, 20

For wisdom will enter your heart, and knowledge will be pleasant to your soul.

Discretion will protect you, and understanding will guard you.

Wisdom will save you from the ways of wicked men, from men whose words are perverse,

Thus you will walk in the ways of good men and keep to the paths of the righteous.

Proverbs 4:14, 15

Do not set foot on the path of the wicked or walk in the way of evil men.

Avoid it, do not travel on it; turn from it and go on your way.

Proverbs 9:6

Leave your simple ways and you will live; walk in the way of understanding.

Proverbs 12:11

He who works his land will have abundant food, but he who chases fantasies lacks judgment.

Proverbs 13:20

He who walks with the wise grows wise, but a companion of fools suffers harm.

Proverbs 14:7

Stay away from a foolish man, for you will not find knowledge on his lips.

Proverbs 14:16

A wise man fears the LORD and shuns evil, but a fool is hotheaded and reckless.

Proverbs 16:17

The highway of the upright avoids evil; he who guards his way guards his life.

Proverbs 16:19

Better to be lowly in spirit and among the oppressed than to share plunder with the proud.

Proverbs 16:29

A violent man entices his neighbor and leads him down a path that is not good.

Proverbs 19:27

Stop listening to instruction, my son, and you will stray from the words of knowledge.

Proverbs 20:19

A gossip betrays a confidence; so avoid a man who talks too much.

Proverbs 22:5

In the paths of the wicked lie thorns and snares, but he who guards his soul stays far from them.

Proverbs 22:24, 25

Do not make friends with a hot-tempered man, do not associate with one easily angered,

or you may learn his ways and get yourself ensnared.

Proverbs 23:6, 7

Do not eat the food of a stingy man, do not crave his delicacies;

for he is the kind of man who is always thinking about the cost. "Eat and drink," he says to you, but his heart is not with you.

Proverbs 23:20, 21

Do not join those who drink too much wine or gorge themselves on meat,

for drunkards and gluttons become poor, and drowsiness clothes them in rags.

Proverbs 24:1

Do not envy wicked men, do not desire their company.

Proverbs 28:4

Those who forsake the law praise the wicked, but those who keep the law resist them.

Proverbs 28:7

He who keeps the law is a discerning son, but a companion of gluttons disgraces his father.

Proverbs 28:19

He who works his land will have abundant food, but the one who chases fantasies will have his fill of poverty.

Proverbs 29:24

The accomplice of a thief is his own enemy; he is put under oath and dare not testify.

Proverbs 29:27

The righteous detest the dishonest; the wicked detest the upright.

BUSYBODY

Proverbs 20:3

It is to a man's honor to avoid strife, but every fool is quick to quarrel.

Proverbs 26:17

Like one who seizes a dog by the ears is a passer-by who meddles in a quarrel not his own.

CONFRONTING

Proverbs 9:8

Do not rebuke a mocker or he will hate you; rebuke a wise man and he will love you.

Proverbs 24:24, 25

Whoever says to the guilty, "You are innocent"-- peoples will curse him and nations denounce him.

But it will go well with those who convict the guilty, and rich blessing will come upon them.

Proverbs 25:9, 10

If you argue your case with a neighbor, do not betray another man's confidence,

or he who hears it may shame you and you will never lose your bad reputation.

Proverbs 25:11

A word aptly spoken is like apples of gold in settings of silver.

Proverbs 25:12

Like an earring of gold or an ornament of fine gold is a wise man's rebuke to a listening ear.

Proverbs 26:17

Like one who seizes a dog by the ears is a passer-by who meddles in a quarrel not his own.

Proverbs 27:17

As iron sharpens iron, so one man sharpens another.

Proverbs 28:4

Those who forsake the law praise the wicked, but those who keep the law resist them.

Proverbs 28:13

He who conceals his sins does not prosper, but whoever confesses and renounces them finds mercy.

Proverbs 28:23

He who rebukes a man will in the end gain more favor than he who has a flattering tongue.

Proverbs 29:27

The righteous detest the dishonest; the wicked detest the upright.

COUNSEL AND ADVICE

Proverbs 1:5

Let the wise listen and add to their learning, and let the discerning get guidance.

Proverbs 8:1, 14

Does not wisdom call out? Does not understanding raise her voice?

Counsel and sound judgment are mine; I have understanding and power.

Proverbs 11:14

For lack of guidance a nation falls, but many advisers make victory sure.

Proverbs 12:5

The plans of the righteous are just, but the advice of the wicked is deceitful.

Proverbs 12:15

The way of a fool seems right to him, but a wise man listens to advice.

Proverbs 12:20

There is deceit in the hearts of those who plot evil, but joy for those who promote peace.

Proverbs 13:10

Pride only breeds quarrels, but wisdom is found in those who take advice.

Proverbs 15:22

Plans fail for lack of counsel, but with many advisers they succeed.

Proverbs 18:13

He who answers before listening--that is his folly and his shame.

Proverbs 19:20

Listen to advice and accept instruction, and in the end you will be wise.

Proverbs 19:21

Many are the plans in a man's heart, but it is the LORD'S purpose that prevails.

Proverbs 20:5

The purposes of a man's heart are deep waters, but a man of understanding draws them out.

Proverbs 20:18

Make plans by seeking advice; if you wage war, obtain guidance.

Proverbs 21:30

There is no wisdom, no insight, no plan that can succeed against the LORD.

Proverbs 24:6

For waging war you need guidance, and for victory many advisers.

Proverbs 25:19

Like a bad tooth or a lame foot is reliance on the unfaithful in times of trouble.

Proverbs 27:9

Perfume and incense bring joy to the heart, and the pleasantness of one's friend springs from his earnest counsel.

Proverbs 27:17

As iron sharpens iron, so one man sharpens another.

GETTING ALONG WITH OTHERS

Proverbs 3:28

Do not say to your neighbor, "Come back later; I'll give it tomorrow"--when you now have it with you.

Proverbs 3:29

Do not plot harm against your neighbor, who lives trustfully near you.

Proverbs 3:30

Do not accuse a man for no reason--when he has done you no harm.

Proverbs 11:12

A man who lacks judgment derides his neighbor, but a man of understanding holds his tongue.

Proverbs 16:7

When a man's ways are pleasing to the LORD, he makes even his enemies live at peace with him.

Proverbs 24:28

Do not testify against your neighbor without cause, or use your lips to deceive.

Proverbs 25:9

If you argue your case with a neighbor, do not betray another man's confidence.

Proverbs 25:17

Seldom set foot in your neighbor's house-- too much of you, and he will hate you.

Proverbs 25:18

Like a club or a sword or a sharp arrow is the man who gives false testimony against his neighbor.

Proverbs 25:20

Like one who takes away a garment on a cold day, or like vinegar poured on soda, is one who sings songs to a heavy heart.

Proverbs 25:21, 22

If your enemy is hungry, give him food to eat; if he is thirsty, give him water to drink.

In doing this, you will heap burning coals on his head, and the LORD will reward you.

Proverbs 26:18, 19

Like a madman shooting firebrands or deadly arrows

is a man who deceives his neighbor and says, "I was only joking!"

Proverbs 27:14

If a man loudly blesses his neighbor early in the morning, it will be taken as a curse.

GOVERNMENT BLESSED

Proverbs 11:10

When the righteous prosper, the city rejoices; when the
wicked perish, there are shouts of joy.

Proverbs 11:11

Through the blessing of the upright a city is exalted, but by
the mouth of the wicked it is destroyed.

Proverbs 14:34

Righteousness exalts a nation, but sin is a disgrace to any
people.

Proverbs 16:12

Kings detest wrongdoing, for a throne is established
through righteousness.

Proverbs 16:13

Kings take pleasure in honest lips; they value a man who
speaks the truth.

Proverbs 20:8

When a king sits on his throne to judge, he winnows out all evil with his eyes.

Proverbs 20:28

Love and faithfulness keep a king safe; through love his throne is made secure.

Proverbs 25:5

Remove the wicked from the king's presence, and his throne will be established through righteousness.

Proverbs 28:2

When a country is rebellious, it has many rulers, but a man of understanding and knowledge maintains order.

Proverbs 29:2

When the righteous thrive, the people rejoice; when the wicked rule, the people groan.

Proverbs 29:8

Mockers stir up a city, but wise men turn away anger.

Proverbs 29:14

If a king judges the poor with fairness, his throne will always be secure.

LOVE AND FRIENDSHIP

Proverbs 3:3

Let love and faithfulness never leave you; bind them around your neck, write them on the tablet of your heart.

Proverbs 9:8

Do not rebuke a mocker or he will hate you; rebuke a wise man and he will love you.

Proverbs 10:12

Hatred stirs up dissension, but love covers over all wrongs.

Proverbs 14:22

Do not those who plot evil go astray? But those who plan what is good find love and faithfulness.

Proverbs 15:17

Better a meal of vegetables where there is love than a fattened calf with hatred.

Proverbs 16:6

Through love and faithfulness sin is atoned for; through the fear of the LORD a man avoids evil.

Proverbs 16:7

When a man's ways are pleasing to the LORD, he makes even his enemies live at peace with him.

Proverbs 17:9

He who covers over an offense promotes love, but whoever repeats the matter separates close friends.

Proverbs 17:17

A friend loves at all times, and a brother is born for adversity.

Proverbs 18:19

An offended brother is more unyielding than a fortified city, and disputes are like the barred gates of a citadel.

Proverbs 18:24

A man of many companions may come to ruin, but there is a friend who sticks closer than a brother.

Proverbs 19:22

What a man desires is unfailing love; better to be poor than a liar.

Proverbs 20:28

Love and faithfulness keep a king safe; through love his throne is made secure.

Proverbs 21:21

He who pursues righteousness and love finds life, prosperity and honor.

Proverbs 22:24

Do not make friends with a hot-tempered man, do not associate with one easily angered.

Proverbs 27:5

Better is open rebuke than hidden love.

Proverbs 27:6

Wounds from a friend can be trusted, but an enemy multiplies kisses.

Proverbs 27:9

Perfume and incense bring joy to the heart, and the pleasantness of one's friend springs from his earnest counsel.

Proverbs 27:10

Do not forsake your friend and the friend of your father, and do not go to your brother's house when disaster strikes you-- better a neighbor nearby than a brother far away.

Proverbs 27:17

As iron sharpens iron, so one man sharpens another.

RESPECT OF PARENTS

Proverbs 1:8, 9

Listen, my son, to your father's instruction and do not forsake your mother's teaching.

They will be a garland to grace your head and a chain to adorn your neck.

Proverbs 4:1, 2

Listen, my sons, to a father's instruction; pay attention and gain understanding.

I give you sound learning, so do not forsake my teaching.

Proverbs 4:10-12

Listen, my son, accept what I say, and the years of your life will be many.

I guide you in the way of wisdom and lead you along straight paths.

When you walk, your steps will not be hampered; when you run, you will not stumble.

Proverbs 4:20-22

My son, pay attention to what I say; listen closely to my words.

Do not let them out of your sight, keep them within your heart;

for they are life to those who find them and health to a man's whole body.

Proverbs 6:20-23

My son, keep your father's commands and do not forsake your mother's teaching.

Bind them upon your heart forever; fasten them around your neck.

When you walk, they will guide you; when you sleep, they will watch over you; when you awake, they will speak to you.

For these commands are a lamp, this teaching is a light, and the corrections of discipline are the way to life,

Proverbs 7:1-3

My son, keep my words and store up my commands within you.

Keep my commands and you will live; guard my teachings as the apple of your eye.

Bind them on your fingers; write them on the tablet of your heart.

Proverbs 10:1

The proverbs of Solomon: A wise son brings joy to his father, but a foolish son grief to his mother.

Proverbs 13:1

A wise son heeds his father's instruction, but a mocker does not listen to rebuke.

Proverbs 15:5

A fool spurns his father's discipline, but whoever heeds correction shows prudence.

Proverbs 15:20

A wise son brings joy to his father, but a foolish man despises his mother.

Proverbs 17:6

Children's children are a crown to the aged, and parents are the pride of their children.

Proverbs 19:26

He who robs his father and drives out his mother is a son who brings shame and disgrace.

Proverbs 20:20

If a man curses his father or mother, his lamp will be snuffed out in pitch darkness.

Proverbs 23:22

Listen to your father, who gave you life, and do not despise your mother when she is old.

Proverbs 23:24, 25

The father of a righteous man has great joy; he who has a wise son delights in him.

May your father and mother be glad; may she who gave you birth rejoice!

Proverbs 23:26

My son, give me your heart and let your eyes keep to my ways.

Proverbs 28:7

He who keeps the law is a discerning son, but a companion of gluttons disgraces his father.

Proverbs 28:24

He who robs his father or mother and says, "It's not wrong"--he is partner to him who destroys.

Proverbs 30:17

The eye that mocks a father, that scorns obedience to a mother, will be pecked out by the ravens of the valley, will be eaten by the vultures.

PART SIX

Wrong Doings

BRIBERY

Proverbs 15:27

A greedy man brings trouble to his family, but he who hates bribes will live.

Proverbs 17:23

A wicked man accepts a bribe in secret to pervert the course of justice.

Proverbs 28:21

To show partiality is not good-- yet a man will do wrong for a piece of bread.

Proverbs 29:4

By justice a king gives a country stability, but one who is greedy for bribes tears it down.

CHEATING AND STEALING

Proverbs 6:30

Men do not despise a thief if he steals to satisfy his hunger when he is starving.

Proverbs 11:1

The LORD abhors dishonest scales, but accurate weights are his delight.

Proverbs 13:11

Dishonest money dwindles away, but he who gathers money little by little makes it grow.

Proverbs 12:22

The LORD detests lying lips, but he delights in men who are truthful.

Proverbs 16:8

Better a little with righteousness than much gain with injustice.

Proverbs 20:23

The LORD detests differing weights, and dishonest scales do not please him.

Proverbs 21:7

The violence of the wicked will drag them away, for they refuse to do what is right.

Proverbs 28:8

He who increases his wealth by exorbitant interest amasses it for another, who will be kind to the poor.

Proverbs 29:24

The accomplice of a thief is his own enemy; he is put under oath and dare not testify.

Proverbs 29:27

The righteous detest the dishonest; the wicked detest the upright.

Proverbs 30:7-9

Two things I ask of you, O LORD; do not refuse me before I die:

Keep falsehood and lies far from me; give me neither poverty nor riches, but give me only my daily bread.

Otherwise, I may have too much and disown you and say, 'Who is the LORD?' Or I may become poor and steal, and so dishonor the name of my God.

CRUELTY

Proverbs 11:17

A kind man benefits himself, but a cruel man brings trouble on himself.

Proverbs 12:10

A righteous man cares for the needs of his animal, but the kindest acts of the wicked are cruel.

Proverbs 17:11

An evil man is bent only on rebellion; a merciless official will be sent against him.

Proverbs 27:4

Anger is cruel and fury overwhelming, but who can stand before jealousy?

EVIL

Proverbs 1:10, 15, 16

My son, if sinners entice you, do not give in to them.

my son, do not go along with them, do not set foot on their paths;

for their feet rush into sin, they are swift to shed blood.

Proverbs 2:11-14

Discretion will protect you, and understanding will guard you.

Wisdom will save you from the ways of wicked men, from men whose words are perverse,

who leave the straight paths to walk in dark ways,

who delight in doing wrong and rejoice in the perverseness of evil.

Proverbs 3:7

Do not be wise in your own eyes; fear the LORD and shun evil.

Proverbs 4:14-17

Do not set foot on the path of the wicked or walk in the way of evil men.

Avoid it, do not travel on it; turn from it and go on your way.

For they cannot sleep till they do evil; they are robbed of slumber till they make someone fall.

They eat the bread of wickedness and drink the wine of violence.

Proverbs 4:27

Do not swerve to the right or the left; keep your foot from evil.

Proverbs 5:22

The evil deeds of a wicked man ensnare him; the cords of his sin hold him fast.

Proverbs 8:13

To fear the LORD is to hate evil; I hate pride and arrogance, evil behavior and perverse speech.

Proverbs 10:23

A fool finds pleasure in evil conduct, but a man of understanding delights in wisdom.

Proverbs 10:29

The way of the LORD is a refuge for the righteous, but it is the ruin of those who do evil.

Proverbs 11:6

The righteousness of the upright delivers them, but the unfaithful are trapped by evil desires.

Proverbs 11:19

The truly righteous man attains life, but he who pursues evil goes to his death.

Proverbs 11:27

He who seeks good finds goodwill, but evil comes to him who searches for it.

Proverbs 12:12

The wicked desire the plunder of evil men, but the root of the righteous flourishes.

Proverbs 12:21

No harm befalls the righteous, but the wicked have their fill of trouble.

Proverbs 13:19

A longing fulfilled is sweet to the soul, but fools detest turning from evil.

Proverbs 13:21

Misfortune pursues the sinner, but prosperity is the reward of the righteous.

Proverbs 14:16

A wise man fears the LORD and shuns evil, but a fool is hotheaded and reckless.

Proverbs 14:19

Evil men will bow down in the presence of the good, and the wicked at the gates of the righteous.

Proverbs 15:3

The eyes of the LORD are everywhere, keeping watch on the wicked and the good.

Proverbs 15:15

All the days of the oppressed are wretched, but the cheerful heart has a continual feast.

Proverbs 15:28

The heart of the righteous weighs its answers, but the mouth of the wicked gushes evil.

Proverbs 16:6

Through love and faithfulness sin is atoned for; through the fear of the LORD a man avoids evil.

Proverbs 16:17

The highway of the upright avoids evil; he who guards his way guards his life.

Proverbs 16:27

A scoundrel plots evil, and his speech is like a scorching fire.

Proverbs 16:29, 30

A violent man entices his neighbor and leads him down a path that is not good.

He who winks with his eye is plotting perversity; he who purses his lips is bent on evil.

Proverbs 17:4

A wicked man listens to evil lips; a liar pays attention to a malicious tongue.

Proverbs 17:11

An evil man is bent only on rebellion; a merciless official will be sent against him.

Proverbs 17:13

If a man pays back evil for good, evil will never leave his house.

Proverbs 19:28

A corrupt witness mocks at justice, and the mouth of the wicked gulps down evil.

Proverbs 20:8

When a king sits on his throne to judge, he winnows out all evil with his eyes.

Proverbs 20:30

Blows and wounds cleanse away evil, and beatings purge the inmost being.

Proverbs 21:10

The wicked man craves evil; his neighbor gets no mercy from him.

Proverbs 22:3; 27:12

A prudent man sees danger and takes refuge, but the simple keep going and suffer for it.

Proverbs 24:20

For the evil man has no future hope, and the lamp of the wicked will be snuffed out.

Proverbs 26:23

Like a coating of glaze over earthenware are fervent lips with an evil heart.

Proverbs 28:5

Evil men do not understand justice, but those who seek the
LORD understand it fully.

Proverbs 28:10

He who leads the upright along an evil path will fall into his
own trap, but the blameless will receive a good inheritance.

Proverbs 29:6

An evil man is snared by his own sin, but a righteous one
can sing and be glad.

EVIL PLANNING

Proverbs 3:29

Do not plot harm against your neighbor, who lives trustfully near you.

Proverbs 6:14

Who plots evil with deceit in his heart--he always stirs up dissension.

Proverbs 6:16, 18

There are six things the LORD hates, seven that are detestable to him:

a heart that devises wicked schemes, feet that are quick to rush into evil.

Proverbs 10:23

A fool finds pleasure in evil conduct, but a man of understanding delights in wisdom.

Proverbs 11:19

The truly righteous man attains life, but he who pursues evil goes to his death.

Proverbs 11:27

He who seeks good finds goodwill, but evil comes to him who searches for it.

Proverbs 12:2

A good man obtains favor from the LORD, but the LORD condemns a crafty man.

Proverbs 12:3

A man cannot be established through wickedness, but the righteous cannot be uprooted.

Proverbs 12:20

There is deceit in the hearts of those who plot evil, but joy for those who promote peace.

Proverbs 14:22

Do not those who plot evil go astray? But those who plan what is good find love and faithfulness.

Proverbs 15:28

The heart of the righteous weighs its answers, but the mouth of the wicked gushes evil.

Proverbs 16:27

A scoundrel plots evil, and his speech is like a scorching fire.

Proverbs 17:13

If a man pays back evil for good, evil will never leave his house.

Proverbs 20:22

Do not say, "I'll pay you back for this wrong!" Wait for the LORD, and he will deliver you.

Proverbs 21:27

The sacrifice of the wicked is detestable-- how much more so when brought with evil intent!

Proverbs 22:8

He who sows wickedness reaps trouble, and the rod of his fury will be destroyed.

Proverbs 24:8

He who plots evil will be known as a schemer.

Proverbs 24:28, 29

Do not testify against your neighbor without cause, or use your lips to deceive.

Do not say, "I'll do to him as he has done to me; I'll pay that man back for what he did."

Proverbs 25:21, 22

If your enemy is hungry, give him food to eat; if he is thirsty, give him water to drink.

In doing this, you will heap burning coals on his head, and the LORD will reward you.

Proverbs 28:10

He who leads the upright along an evil path will fall into his own trap, but the blameless will receive a good inheritance.

Proverbs 30:32

If you have played the fool and exalted yourself, or if you have planned evil, clap your hand over your mouth!

EVIL THINKING

Proverbs 6:16, 18

There are six things the LORD hates, seven that are detestable to him:

a heart that devises wicked schemes, feet that are quick to rush into evil.

Proverbs 12:13

An evil man is trapped by his sinful talk, but a righteous man escapes trouble.

Proverbs 15:28

The heart of the righteous weighs its answers, but the mouth of the wicked gushes evil.

MISCHIEF

Proverbs 10:23

A fool finds pleasure in evil conduct, but a man of understanding delights in wisdom.

Proverbs 15:21

Folly delights a man who lacks judgment, but a man of understanding keeps a straight course.

Proverbs 17:20

A man of perverse heart does not prosper; he whose tongue is deceitful falls into trouble.

Proverbs 24:1, 2

Do not envy wicked men, do not desire their company;

for their hearts plot violence, and their lips talk about making trouble.

Proverbs 24:8

He who plots evil will be known as a schemer.

Proverbs 26:18, 19

Like a madman shooting firebrands or deadly arrows

is a man who deceives his neighbor and says, "I was only joking!"

REJOICING IN EVIL

Proverbs 17:5

He who mocks the poor shows contempt for their Maker;
whoever gloats over disaster will not go unpunished.

Proverbs 24:17, 18

Do not gloat when your enemy falls; when he stumbles, do
not let your heart rejoice,

or the LORD will see and disapprove and turn his wrath
away from him.

SCORN
(MOCKERY)

Proverbs 1:20, 22

Wisdom calls aloud in the street, she raises her voice in the public squares;

How long will you simple ones love your simple ways? How long will mockers delight in mockery and fools hate knowledge?

Proverbs 3:34

He mocks proud mockers but gives grace to the humble.

Proverbs 9:7

Whoever corrects a mocker invites insult; whoever rebukes a wicked man incurs abuse.

Proverbs 9:8

Do not rebuke a mocker or he will hate you; rebuke a wise man and he will love you.

Proverbs 9:12

If you are wise, your wisdom will reward you; if you are a mocker, you alone will suffer.

Proverbs 13:1

A wise son heeds his father's instruction, but a mocker does not listen to rebuke.

Proverbs 14:6

The mocker seeks wisdom and finds none, but knowledge comes easily to the discerning.

Proverbs 15:12

A mocker resents correction; he will not consult the wise.

Proverbs 17:5

He who mocks the poor shows contempt for their Maker; whoever gloats over disaster will not go unpunished.

Proverbs 19:25

Flog a mocker, and the simple will learn prudence; rebuke a discerning man, and he will gain knowledge.

Proverbs 19:28

A corrupt witness mocks at justice, and the mouth of the wicked gulps down evil.

Proverbs 19:29

Penalties are prepared for mockers, and beatings for the backs of fools.

Proverbs 21:11

When a mocker is punished, the simple gain wisdom; when a wise man is instructed, he gets knowledge.

Proverbs 21:24

The proud and arrogant man--"Mocker" is his name; he behaves with overweening pride.

Proverbs 22:10

Drive out the mocker, and out goes strife; quarrels and insults are ended.

Proverbs 24:9

The schemes of folly are sin, and men detest a mocker.

Proverbs 29:8

Mockers stir up a city, but wise men turn away anger.

Proverbs 30:17

The eye that mocks a father, that scorns obedience to a mother, will be pecked out by the ravens of the valley, will be eaten by the vultures.

VENGEANCE

Proverbs 11:31

If the righteous receive their due on earth, how much more
the ungodly and the sinner!

Proverbs 20:22

Do not say, "I'll pay you back for this wrong!" Wait for the
LORD, and he will deliver you.

Proverbs 24:28, 29

Do not testify against your neighbor without cause, or use
your lips to deceive.

Do not say, "I'll do to him as he has done to me; I'll pay that
man back for what he did."

Proverbs 25:21, 22

If your enemy is hungry, give him food to eat; if he is
thirsty, give him water to drink.

In doing this, you will heap burning coals on his head, and
the LORD will reward you.

WICKEDNESS

Proverbs 2:12

Wisdom will save you from the ways of wicked men, from men whose words are perverse.

Proverbs 2:22

But the wicked will be cut off from the land, and the unfaithful will be torn from it.

Proverbs 3:25

Have no fear of sudden disaster or of the ruin that overtakes the wicked.

Proverbs 3:33

The LORD'S curse is on the house of the wicked, but he blesses the home of the righteous.

Proverbs 4:14

Do not set foot on the path of the wicked or walk in the way of evil men.

Proverbs 4:14, 17

Do not set foot on the path of the wicked or walk in the way of evil men.

They eat the bread of wickedness and drink the wine of violence.

Proverbs 4:19

But the way of the wicked is like deep darkness; they do not know what makes them stumble.

Proverbs 5:22, 23

The evil deeds of a wicked man ensnare him; the cords of his sin hold him fast.

He will die for lack of discipline, led astray by his own great folly.

Proverbs 6:12-15

A scoundrel and villain, who goes about with a corrupt mouth,

who winks with his eye, signals with his feet and motions with his fingers,

who plots evil with deceit in his heart--he always stirs up dissension.

Therefore disaster will overtake him in an instant; he will suddenly be destroyed--without remedy.

Proverbs 8:1, 7

Does not wisdom call out? Does not understanding raise her voice?

My mouth speaks what is true, for my lips detest wickedness.

Proverbs 10:2

Ill-gotten treasures are of no value, but righteousness delivers from death.

Proverbs 10:3

The LORD does not let the righteous go hungry but he thwarts the craving of the wicked.

Proverbs 10:6

Blessings crown the head of the righteous, but violence overwhelms the mouth of the wicked.

Proverbs 10:7

The memory of the righteous will be a blessing, but the name of the wicked will rot.

Proverbs 10:11

The mouth of the righteous is a fountain of life, but violence overwhelms the mouth of the wicked.

Proverbs 10:16

The wages of the righteous bring them life, but the income of the wicked brings them punishment.

Proverbs 10:20

The tongue of the righteous is choice silver, but the heart of the wicked is of little value.

Proverbs 10:24

What the wicked dreads will overtake him; what the righteous desire will be granted.

Proverbs 10:25

When the storm has swept by, the wicked are gone, but the righteous stand firm forever.

Proverbs 10:27

The fear of the LORD adds length to life, but the years of the wicked are cut short.

Proverbs 10:28

The prospect of the righteous is joy, but the hopes of the wicked come to nothing.

Proverbs 10:29

The way of the LORD is a refuge for the righteous, but it is the ruin of those who do evil.

Proverbs 10:30

The righteous will never be uprooted, but the wicked will not remain in the land.

Proverbs 10:32

The lips of the righteous know what is fitting, but the mouth of the wicked only what is perverse.

Proverbs 11:5

The righteousness of the blameless makes a straight way for them, but the wicked are brought down by their own wickedness.

Proverbs 11:7

When a wicked man dies, his hope perishes; all he expected from his power comes to nothing.

Proverbs 11:8

The righteous man is rescued from trouble, and it comes on the wicked instead.

Proverbs 11:10

When the righteous prosper, the city rejoices; when the wicked perish, there are shouts of joy.

Proverbs 11:11

Through the blessing of the upright a city is exalted, but by the mouth of the wicked it is destroyed.

Proverbs 11:18

The wicked man earns deceptive wages, but he who sows righteousness reaps a sure reward.

Proverbs 11:21

Be sure of this: The wicked will not go unpunished, but those who are righteous will go free.

Proverbs 11:23

The desire of the righteous ends only in good, but the hope of the wicked only in wrath.

Proverbs 12:3

A man cannot be established through wickedness, but the righteous cannot be uprooted.

Proverbs 12:5

The plans of the righteous are just, but the advice of the wicked is deceitful.

Proverbs 12:6

The words of the wicked lie in wait for blood, but the speech of the upright rescues them.

Proverbs 12:7

Wicked men are overthrown and are no more, but the house of the righteous stands firm.

Proverbs 12:10

A righteous man cares for the needs of his animal, but the kindest acts of the wicked are cruel.

Proverbs 12:12

The wicked desire the plunder of evil men, but the root of the righteous flourishes.

Proverbs 12:21

No harm befalls the righteous, but the wicked have their fill of trouble.

Proverbs 12:26

A righteous man is cautious in friendship, but the way of the wicked leads them astray.

Proverbs 13:5

The righteous hate what is false, but the wicked bring shame and disgrace.

Proverbs 13:6

Righteousness guards the man of integrity, but wickedness overthrows the sinner.

Proverbs 13:9

The light of the righteous shines brightly, but the lamp of the wicked is snuffed out.

Proverbs 13:17

A wicked messenger falls into trouble, but a trustworthy envoy brings healing.

Proverbs 13:25

The righteous eat to their hearts' content, but the stomach of the wicked goes hungry.

Proverbs 14:11

The house of the wicked will be destroyed, but the tent of the upright will flourish.

Proverbs 14:19

Evil men will bow down in the presence of the good, and the wicked at the gates of the righteous.

Proverbs 14:32

When calamity comes, the wicked are brought down, but even in death the righteous have a refuge.

Proverbs 15:3

The eyes of the LORD are everywhere, keeping watch on the wicked and the good.

Proverbs 15:6

The house of the righteous contains great treasure, but the income of the wicked brings them trouble.

Proverbs 15:8

The LORD detests the sacrifice of the wicked, but the prayer of the upright pleases him.

Proverbs 15:9

The LORD detests the way of the wicked but he loves those who pursue righteousness.

Proverbs 15:26

The LORD detests the thoughts of the wicked, but those of the pure are pleasing to him.

Proverbs 15:28

The heart of the righteous weighs its answers, but the mouth of the wicked gushes evil.

Proverbs 15:29

The LORD is far from the wicked but he hears the prayer of the righteous.

Proverbs 16:4

The LORD works out everything for his own ends-- even the wicked for a day of disaster.

Proverbs 17:4

A wicked man listens to evil lips; a liar pays attention to a malicious tongue.

Proverbs 17:23

A wicked man accepts a bribe in secret to pervert the course of justice.

Proverbs 18:3

When wickedness comes, so does contempt, and with shame comes disgrace.

Proverbs 18:5

It is not good to be partial to the wicked or to deprive the innocent of justice.

Proverbs 19:28

A corrupt witness mocks at justice, and the mouth of the wicked gulps down evil.

Proverbs 20:26

A wise king winnows out the wicked; he drives the threshing wheel over them.

Proverbs 21:4

Haughty eyes and a proud heart, the lamp of the wicked, are sin!

Proverbs 21:7

The violence of the wicked will drag them away, for they refuse to do what is right.

Proverbs 21:10

The wicked man craves evil; his neighbor gets no mercy
from him.

Proverbs 21:12

The Righteous One takes note of the house of the wicked
and brings the wicked to ruin.

Proverbs 21:18

The wicked become a ransom for the righteous, and the
unfaithful for the upright.

Proverbs 21:27

The sacrifice of the wicked is detestable-- how much more
so when brought with evil intent!

Proverbs 21:29

A wicked man puts up a bold front, but an upright man
gives thought to his ways.

Proverbs 22:5

In the paths of the wicked lie thorns and snares, but he who
guards his soul stays far from them.

Proverbs 22:8

He who sows wickedness reaps trouble, and the rod of his
fury will be destroyed.

Proverbs 24:16

For though a righteous man falls seven times, he rises again,
but the wicked are brought down by calamity.

Proverbs 24:19, 20

Do not fret because of evil men or be envious of the
wicked,

for the evil man has no future hope, and the lamp of the
wicked will be snuffed out.

Proverbs 25:5

Remove the wicked from the king's presence, and his throne
will be established through righteousness.

Proverbs 25:26

Like a muddied spring or a polluted well is a righteous man
who gives way to the wicked.

Proverbs 26:23

Like a coating of glaze over earthenware are fervent lips
with an evil heart.

Proverbs 26:24, 26

A malicious man disguises himself with his lips, but in his
heart he harbors deceit.

His malice may be concealed by deception, but his wickedness will be exposed in the assembly.

Proverbs 28:1

The wicked man flees though no one pursues, but the righteous are as bold as a lion.

Proverbs 28:4

Those who forsake the law praise the wicked, but those who keep the law resist them.

Proverbs 28:12

When the righteous triumph, there is great elation; but when the wicked rise to power, men go into hiding.

Proverbs 28:15

Like a roaring lion or a charging bear is a wicked man ruling over a helpless people.

Proverbs 28:28

When the wicked rise to power, people go into hiding; but when the wicked perish, the righteous thrive.

Proverbs 29:2

When the righteous thrive, the people rejoice; when the wicked rule, the people groan.

Proverbs 29:7

The righteous care about justice for the poor, but the wicked have no such concern.

Proverbs 29:12

If a ruler listens to lies, all his officials become wicked.

Proverbs 29:16

When the wicked thrive, so does sin, but the righteous will see their downfall.

Proverbs 29:27

The righteous detest the dishonest; the wicked detest the upright.

PART SEVEN

Godly Characteristics

DISCRETION AND PRUDENCE

Proverbs 1:1, 3, 4

The proverbs of Solomon son of David, king of Israel:

for acquiring a disciplined and prudent life, doing what is right and just and fair;

For giving prudence to the simple, knowledge and discretion to the young.

Proverbs 2:10-12

For wisdom will enter your heart, and knowledge will be pleasant to your soul.

Discretion will protect you, and understanding will guard you.

Wisdom will save you from the ways of wicked men, from men whose words are perverse.

Proverbs 3:21

My son, preserve sound judgment and discernment, do not let them out of your sight.

257

Proverbs 5:1, 2

My son, pay attention to my wisdom, listen well to my words of insight,

that you may maintain discretion and your lips may preserve knowledge.

Proverbs 8:5

You who are simple, gain prudence; you who are foolish, gain understanding.

Proverbs 8:12

I, wisdom, dwell together with prudence; I possess knowledge and discretion.

Proverbs 11:22

Like a gold ring in a pig's snout is a beautiful woman who shows no discretion.

Proverbs 12:5

The plans of the righteous are just, but the advice of the wicked is deceitful.

Proverbs 12:16

A fool shows his annoyance at once, but a prudent man overlooks an insult.

Proverbs 12:23

A prudent man keeps his knowledge to himself, but the heart of fools blurts out folly.

Proverbs 13:16

Every prudent man acts out of knowledge, but a fool exposes his folly.

Proverbs 14:8

The wisdom of the prudent is to give thought to their ways, but the folly of fools is deception.

Proverbs 14:15

A simple man believes anything, but a prudent man gives thought to his steps.

Proverbs 14:18

The simple inherit folly, but the prudent are crowned with knowledge.

Proverbs 15:5

A fool spurns his father's discipline, but whoever heeds correction shows prudence.

Proverbs 16:21

The wise in heart are called discerning, and pleasant words promote instruction.

Proverbs 18:15

The heart of the discerning acquires knowledge; the ears of the wise seek it out.

Proverbs 19:11

A man's wisdom gives him patience; it is to his glory to overlook an offense.

Proverbs 19:14

Houses and wealth are inherited from parents, but a prudent wife is from the LORD.

Proverbs 19:25

Flog a mocker, and the simple will learn prudence; rebuke a discerning man, and he will gain knowledge.

Proverbs 19:27

Stop listening to instruction, my son, and you will stray from the words of knowledge.

Proverbs 21:5

The plans of the diligent lead to profit as surely as haste leads to poverty.

Proverbs 22:3; 27:12

A prudent man sees danger and takes refuge, but the simple keep going and suffer for it.

FAITHFULNESS

Proverbs 2:8

For he guards the course of the just and protects the way of his faithful ones.

Proverbs 3:3

Let love and faithfulness never leave you; bind them around your neck, write them on the tablet of your heart.

Proverbs 11:13

A gossip betrays a confidence, but a trustworthy man keeps a secret.

Proverbs 13:17

A wicked messenger falls into trouble, but a trustworthy envoy brings healing.

Proverbs 14:5

A truthful witness does not deceive, but a false witness pours out lies.

Proverbs 14:22

Do not those who plot evil go astray? But those who plan what is good find love and faithfulness.

Proverbs 20:6

Many a man claims to have unfailing love, but a faithful man who can find?

Proverbs 20:28

Love and faithfulness keep a king safe; through love his throne is made secure.

Proverbs 25:13

Like the coolness of snow at harvest time is a trustworthy messenger to those who send him; he refreshes the spirit of his masters.

Proverbs 25:19

Like a bad tooth or a lame foot is reliance on the unfaithful in times of trouble.

Proverbs 28:20

A faithful man will be richly blessed, but one eager to get rich will not go unpunished.

Proverbs 29:14

If a king judges the poor with fairness, his throne will always be secure.

GOODNESS

Proverbs 2:1, 9

My son, if you accept my words and store up my commands within you,

Then you will understand what is right and just and fair--every good path.

Proverbs 2:20

Thus you will walk in the ways of good men and keep to the paths of the righteous.

Proverbs 3:4

Then you will win favor and a good name in the sight of God and man.

Proverbs 3:27

Do not withhold good from those who deserve it, when it is in your power to act.

Proverbs 11:17

A kind man benefits himself, but a cruel man brings trouble on himself.

Proverbs 11:23

The desire of the righteous ends only in good, but the hope of the wicked only in wrath.

Proverbs 11:27

He who seeks good finds goodwill, but evil comes to him who searches for it.

Proverbs 12:2

A good man obtains favor from the LORD, but the LORD condemns a crafty man.

Proverbs 12:25

An anxious heart weighs a man down, but a kind word cheers him up.

Proverbs 13:22

A good man leaves an inheritance for his children's children, but a sinner's wealth is stored up for the righteous.

Proverbs 14:14

The faithless will be fully repaid for their ways, and the good man rewarded for his.

Proverbs 14:19

Evil men will bow down in the presence of the good, and the wicked at the gates of the righteous.

Proverbs 14:22

Do not those who plot evil go astray? But those who plan what is good find love and faithfulness.

Proverbs 17:20

A man of perverse heart does not prosper; he whose tongue is deceitful falls into trouble.

Proverbs 17:26

It is not good to punish an innocent man, or to flog officials for their integrity.

Proverbs 18:5

It is not good to be partial to the wicked or to deprive the innocent of justice.

Proverbs 19:8

He who gets wisdom loves his own soul; he who cherishes understanding prospers.

Proverbs 22:1

A good name is more desirable than great riches; to be esteemed is better than silver or gold.

Proverbs 24:23

These also are sayings of the wise: To show partiality in judging is not good.

Proverbs 28:21

To show partiality is not good-- yet a man will do wrong for a piece of bread.

HAPPINESS

Proverbs 3:13, 18

Blessed is the man who finds wisdom, the man who gains understanding,

She is a tree of life to those who embrace her; those who lay hold of her will be blessed.

Proverbs 8:32

Now then, my sons, listen to me; blessed are those who keep my ways.

Proverbs 8:34

Blessed is the man who listens to me, watching daily at my doors, waiting at my doorway.

Proverbs 12:25

An anxious heart weighs a man down, but a kind word cheers him up.

Proverbs 14:21

He who despises his neighbor sins, but blessed is he who is kind to the needy.

Proverbs 15:13

A happy heart makes the face cheerful, but heartache crushes the spirit.

Proverbs 15:15

All the days of the oppressed are wretched, but the cheerful heart has a continual feast.

Proverbs 15:30

A cheerful look brings joy to the heart, and good news gives health to the bones.

Proverbs 16:20

Whoever gives heed to instruction prospers, and blessed is he who trusts in the LORD.

Proverbs 17:22

A cheerful heart is good medicine, but a crushed spirit dries up the bones.

Proverbs 22:9

A generous man will himself be blessed, for he shares his food with the poor.

Proverbs 28:14

Blessed is the man who always fears the LORD, but he who hardens his heart falls into trouble.

Proverbs 28:20

A faithful man will be richly blessed, but one eager to get rich will not go unpunished.

Proverbs 29:18

Where there is no revelation, the people cast off restraint; but blessed is he who keeps the law.

HONESTY

Proverbs 2:7

He holds victory in store for the upright, he is a shield to
those whose walk is blameless.

Proverbs 2:21

For the upright will live in the land, and the blameless will
remain in it.

Proverbs 10:9

The man of integrity walks securely, but he who takes
crooked paths will be found out.

Proverbs 11:1

The LORD abhors dishonest scales, but accurate weights
are his delight.

Proverbs 11:3

The integrity of the upright guides them, but the unfaithful
are destroyed by their duplicity.

271

Proverbs 11:5

The righteousness of the blameless makes a straight way for them, but the wicked are brought down by their own wickedness.

Proverbs 11:20

The LORD detests men of perverse heart but he delights in those whose ways are blameless.

Proverbs 12:17

A truthful witness gives honest testimony, but a false witness tells lies.

Proverbs 12:19

Truthful lips endure forever, but a lying tongue lasts only a moment.

Proverbs 12:22

The LORD detests lying lips, but he delights in men who are truthful.

Proverbs 13:5

The righteous hate what is false, but the wicked bring shame and disgrace.

Proverbs 13:6

Righteousness guards the man of integrity, but wickedness overthrows the sinner.

Proverbs 14:25

A truthful witness saves lives, but a false witness is deceitful.

Proverbs 16:11

Honest scales and balances are from the LORD; all the weights in the bag are of his making.

Proverbs 16:13

Kings take pleasure in honest lips; they value a man who speaks the truth.

Proverbs 17:15

Acquitting the guilty and condemning the innocent--the LORD detests them both.

Proverbs 19:1

Better a poor man whose walk is blameless than a fool whose lips are perverse.

Proverbs 20:7

The righteous man leads a blameless life; blessed are his children after him.

Proverbs 20:10

Differing weights and differing measures--the LORD detests them both.

Proverbs 20:23

The LORD detests differing weights, and dishonest scales do not please him.

Proverbs 21:3

To do what is right and just is more acceptable to the LORD than sacrifice.

Proverbs 24:11, 12

Rescue those being led away to death; hold back those staggering toward slaughter.

If you say, "But we knew nothing about this," does not he who weighs the heart perceive it? Does not he who guards your life know it? Will he not repay each person according to what he has done?

Proverbs 24:26

An honest answer is like a kiss on the lips.

Proverbs 24:28, 29

Do not testify against your neighbor without cause, or use your lips to deceive.

Do not say, "I'll do to him as he has done to me; I'll pay that man back for what he did."

Proverbs 28:6

Better a poor man whose walk is blameless than a rich man whose ways are perverse.

Proverbs 28:8

He who increases his wealth by exorbitant interest amasses it for another, who will be kind to the poor.

Proverbs 28:10

He who leads the upright along an evil path will fall into his own trap, but the blameless will receive a good inheritance.

Proverbs 28:13

He who conceals his sins does not prosper, but whoever confesses and renounces them finds mercy.

Proverbs 28:18

He whose walk is blameless is kept safe, but he whose ways are perverse will suddenly fall.

Proverbs 29:10

Bloodthirsty men hate a man of integrity and seek to kill the upright.

HUMILITY

Proverbs 3:34

He mocks proud mockers but gives grace to the humble.

Proverbs 11:2

When pride comes, then comes disgrace, but with humility comes wisdom.

Proverbs 15:33

The fear of the LORD teaches a man wisdom, AND humility comes before honor.

Proverbs 16:19

Better to be lowly in spirit and among the oppressed than to share plunder with the proud.

Proverbs 18:12

Before his downfall a man's heart is proud, but humility comes before honor.

Proverbs 22:4

Humility and the fear of the LORD bring wealth and honor and life.

Proverbs 25:6, 7

Do not exalt yourself in the king's presence, and do not claim a place among great men;

it is better for him to say to you, "Come up here," than for him to humiliate you before a nobleman.

Proverbs 29:23

A man's pride brings him low, but a man of lowly spirit gains honor.

JUSTNESS

Proverbs 1:1, 3

The proverbs of Solomon son of David, king of Israel:

For acquiring a disciplined and prudent life, doing what is right and just and fair.

Proverbs 2:6, 8, 9

For the LORD gives wisdom, and from his mouth come knowledge and understanding.

Then you will understand what is right and just and fair-- every good path.

For he guards the course of the just and protects the way of his faithful ones.

Proverbs 8:8

All the words of my mouth are just; none of them is crooked or perverse.

Proverbs 8:1, 15, 20

Does not wisdom call out? Does not understanding raise her voice?

By me kings reign and rulers make laws that are just.
I walk in the way of righteousness, along the paths of justice.

Proverbs 12:5

The plans of the righteous are just, but the advice of the wicked is deceitful.

Proverbs 16:10

The lips of a king speak as an oracle, and his mouth should not betray justice.

Proverbs 16:11

Honest scales and balances are from the LORD; all the weights in the bag are of his making.

Proverbs 17:15

Acquitting the guilty and condemning the innocent--the LORD detests them both.

Proverbs 17:23

A wicked man accepts a bribe in secret to pervert the course of justice.

Proverbs 17:26

It is not good to punish an innocent man, or to flog officials for their integrity.

Proverbs 18:5

It is not good to be partial to the wicked or to deprive the innocent of justice.

Proverbs 19:28

A corrupt witness mocks at justice, and the mouth of the wicked gulps down evil.

Proverbs 21:3

To do what is right and just is more acceptable to the LORD than sacrifice.

Proverbs 21:15

When justice is done, it brings joy to the righteous but terror to evildoers.

Proverbs 24:16

For though a righteous man falls seven times, he rises again, but the wicked are brought down by calamity.

Proverbs 28:5

Evil men do not understand justice, but those who seek the LORD understand it fully.

Proverbs 29:4

By justice a king gives a country stability, but one who is greedy for bribes tears it down.

Proverbs 29:7

The righteous care about justice for the poor, but the wicked have no such concern.

Proverbs 29:26

Many seek an audience with a ruler, but it is from the LORD that man gets justice.

Proverbs 31:8, 9

"Speak up for those who cannot speak for themselves, for the rights of all who are destitute.

Speak up and judge fairly; defend the rights of the poor and needy."

MERCY

Proverbs 11:16

A kindhearted woman gains respect, but ruthless men gain only wealth.

Proverbs 11:17

A kind man benefits himself, but a cruel man brings trouble on himself.

Proverbs 14:21

He who despises his neighbor sins, but blessed is he who is kind to the needy.

Proverbs 14:31

He who oppresses the poor shows contempt for their Maker, but whoever is kind to the needy honors God.

Proverbs 18:23

A poor man pleads for mercy, but a rich man answers harshly.

Proverbs 19:17

He who is kind to the poor lends to the LORD, and he will reward him for what he has done.

Proverbs 21:10

The wicked man craves evil; his neighbor gets no mercy from him.

Proverbs 28:8

He who increases his wealth by exorbitant interest amasses it for another, who will be kind to the poor.

Proverbs 28:13

He who conceals his sins does not prosper, but whoever confesses and renounces them finds mercy.

RIGHTEOUSNESS

Proverbs 2:20

Thus you will walk in the ways of good men and keep to the paths of the righteous.

Proverbs 3:33

The LORD'S curse is on the house of the wicked, but he blesses the home of the righteous.

Proverbs 4:18

The path of the righteous is like the first gleam of dawn, shining ever brighter till the full light of day.

Proverbs 8:20

I walk in the way of righteousness, along the paths of justice.

Proverbs 9:9

Instruct a wise man and he will be wiser still; teach a righteous man and he will add to his learning.

Proverbs 10:2

Ill-gotten treasures are of no value, but righteousness delivers from death.

Proverbs 10:3

The LORD does not let the righteous go hungry but he thwarts the craving of the wicked.

Proverbs 10:6

Blessings crown the head of the righteous, but violence overwhelms the mouth of the wicked.

Proverbs 10:7

The memory of the righteous will be a blessing, but the name of the wicked will rot.

Proverbs 10:11

The mouth of the righteous is a fountain of life, but violence overwhelms the mouth of the wicked.

Proverbs 10:16

The wages of the righteous bring them life, but the income of the wicked brings them punishment.

Proverbs 10:20

The tongue of the righteous is choice silver, but the heart of the wicked is of little value.

Proverbs 10:21

The lips of the righteous nourish many, but fools die for lack of judgment.

Proverbs 10:24

What the wicked dreads will overtake him; what the righteous desire will be granted.

Proverbs 10:25

When the storm has swept by, the wicked are gone, but the righteous stand firm forever.

Proverbs 10:28

The prospect of the righteous is joy, but the hopes of the wicked come to nothing.

Proverbs 10:29

The way of the LORD is a refuge for the righteous, but it is the ruin of those who do evil.

Proverbs 10:30

The righteous will never be uprooted, but the wicked will not remain in the land.

Proverbs 10:31

The mouth of the righteous brings forth wisdom, but a perverse tongue will be cut out.

Proverbs 10:32

The lips of the righteous know what is fitting, but the mouth of the wicked only what is perverse.

Proverbs 11:4

Wealth is worthless in the day of wrath, but righteousness delivers from death.

Proverbs 11:5

The righteousness of the blameless makes a straight way for them, but the wicked are brought down by their own wickedness.

Proverbs 11:6

The righteousness of the upright delivers them, but the unfaithful are trapped by evil desires.

Proverbs 11:8

The righteous man is rescued from trouble, and it comes on the wicked instead.

Proverbs 11:9

With his mouth the godless destroys his neighbor, but through knowledge the righteous escape.

Proverbs 11:10

When the righteous prosper, the city rejoices; when the wicked perish, there are shouts of joy.

Proverbs 11:18

The wicked man earns deceptive wages, but he who sows righteousness reaps a sure reward.

Proverbs 11:19

The truly righteous man attains life, but he who pursues evil goes to his death.

Proverbs 11:21

Be sure of this: The wicked will not go unpunished, but those who are righteous will go free.

Proverbs 11:23

The desire of the righteous ends only in good, but the hope of the wicked only in wrath.

Proverbs 11:28

Whoever trusts in his riches will fall, but the righteous will thrive like a green leaf.

Proverbs 11:30

The fruit of the righteous is a tree of life, and he who wins souls is wise.

Proverbs 11:31

If the righteous receive their due on earth, how much more the ungodly and the sinner!

Proverbs 12:3

A man cannot be established through wickedness, but the righteous cannot be uprooted.

Proverbs 12:5

The plans of the righteous are just, but the advice of the wicked is deceitful.

Proverbs 12:7

Wicked men are overthrown and are no more, but the house of the righteous stands firm.

Proverbs 12:10

A righteous man cares for the needs of his animal, but the kindest acts of the wicked are cruel.

Proverbs 12:12

The wicked desire the plunder of evil men, but the root of the righteous flourishes.

Proverbs 12:13

An evil man is trapped by his sinful talk, but a righteous man escapes trouble.

Proverbs 12:21

No harm befalls the righteous, but the wicked have their fill of trouble.

Proverbs 12:26

A righteous man is cautious in friendship, but the way of the wicked leads them astray.

Proverbs 12:28

In the way of righteousness there is life; along that path is immortality.

Proverbs 13:5

The righteous hate what is false, but the wicked bring shame and disgrace.

Proverbs 13:6

Righteousness guards the man of integrity, but wickedness overthrows the sinner.

Proverbs 13:9

The light of the righteous shines brightly, but the lamp of the wicked is snuffed out.

Proverbs 13:21

Misfortune pursues the sinner, but prosperity is the reward of the righteous.

Proverbs 13:25

The righteous eat to their hearts' content, but the stomach of the wicked goes hungry.

Proverbs 14:19

Evil men will bow down in the presence of the good, and the wicked at the gates of the righteous.

Proverbs 14:32

When calamity comes, the wicked are brought down, but even in death the righteous have a refuge.

Proverbs 14:34

Righteousness exalts a nation, but sin is a disgrace to any people.

Proverbs 15:6

The house of the righteous contains great treasure, but the income of the wicked brings them trouble.

Proverbs 15:9

The LORD detests the way of the wicked but he loves those who pursue righteousness.

Proverbs 15:28

The heart of the righteous weighs its answers, but the mouth of the wicked gushes evil.

Proverbs 15:29

The LORD is far from the wicked but he hears the prayer of the righteous.

Proverbs 16:8

Better a little with righteousness than much gain with injustice.

Proverbs 16:12

Kings detest wrongdoing, for a throne is established through righteousness.

Proverbs 16:31

Gray hair is a crown of splendor; it is attained by a righteous life.

Proverbs 18:10

The name of the LORD is a strong tower; the righteous run to it and are safe.

Proverbs 20:7

The righteous man leads a blameless life; blessed are his children after him.

Proverbs 21:12

The Righteous One takes note of the house of the wicked and brings the wicked to ruin.

Proverbs 21:15

When justice is done, it brings joy to the righteous but terror to evildoers.

Proverbs 21:18

The wicked become a ransom for the righteous, and the unfaithful for the upright.

Proverbs 21:21

He who pursues righteousness and love finds life, prosperity and honor.

Proverbs 21:25, 26

The sluggard's craving will be the death of him, because his hands refuse to work.

All day long he craves for more, but the righteous give without sparing.

Proverbs 23:24

The father of a righteous man has great joy; he who has a wise son delights in him.

Proverbs 24:15, 16

Do not lie in wait like an outlaw against a righteous man's house, do not raid his dwelling place.

For though a righteous man falls seven times, he rises again, but the wicked are brought down by calamity.

Proverbs 25:5

Remove the wicked from the king's presence, and his throne will be established through righteousness.

Proverbs 25:26

Like a muddied spring or a polluted well is a righteous man
who gives way to the wicked.

Proverbs 28:1

The wicked man flees though no one pursues, but the
righteous are as bold as a lion.

Proverbs 28:12

When the righteous triumph, there is great elation; but when
the wicked rise to power, men go into hiding.

Proverbs 28:28

When the wicked rise to power, people go into hiding; but
when the wicked perish, the righteous thrive.

Proverbs 29:2

When the righteous thrive, the people rejoice; when the
wicked rule, the people groan.

Proverbs 29:6

An evil man is snared by his own sin, but a righteous one
can sing and be glad.

Proverbs 29:7

The righteous care about justice for the poor, but the wicked
have no such concern.

Proverbs 29:16

When the wicked thrive, so does sin, but the righteous will
see their downfall.

Proverbs 29:27

The righteous detest the dishonest; the wicked detest the
upright.

STRENGTH

Proverbs 5:7, 8, 9

Now then, my sons, listen to me; do not turn aside from what I say.

Keep to a path far from her, do not go near the door of her house,

lest you give your best strength to others and your years to one who is cruel.

Proverbs 10:29

The way of the LORD is a refuge for the righteous, but it is the ruin of those who do evil.

Proverbs 20:29

The glory of young men is their strength, gray hair the splendor of the old.

Proverbs 24:5

A wise man has great power, and a man of knowledge increases strength.

Proverbs 24:10

If you falter in times of trouble, how small is your strength!

Proverbs 31:3

Do not spend your strength on women, your vigor on those who ruin kings.

UPRIGHTNESS

Proverbs 2:7

He holds victory in store for the upright, he is a shield to those whose walk is blameless.

Proverbs 2:21, 22

For the upright will live in the land, and the blameless will remain in it;

but the wicked will be cut off from the land, and the unfaithful will be torn from it.

Proverbs 3:32

For the LORD detests a perverse man but takes the upright into his confidence.

Proverbs 11:3

The integrity of the upright guides them, but the unfaithful are destroyed by their duplicity.

Proverbs 11:6

The righteousness of the upright delivers them, but the unfaithful are trapped by evil desires.

Proverbs 11:11

Through the blessing of the upright a city is exalted, but by the mouth of the wicked it is destroyed.

Proverbs 12:6

The words of the wicked lie in wait for blood, but the speech of the upright rescues them.

Proverbs 14:2

He whose walk is upright fears the LORD, but he whose ways are devious despises him.

Proverbs 14:9

Fools mock at making amends for sin, but goodwill is found among the upright.

Proverbs 14:11

The house of the wicked will be destroyed, but the tent of the upright will flourish.

Proverbs 15:8

The LORD detests the sacrifice of the wicked, but the prayer of the upright pleases him.

Proverbs 15:19

The way of the sluggard is blocked with thorns, but the path of the upright is a highway.

Proverbs 16:17

The highway of the upright avoids evil; he who guards his way guards his life.

Proverbs 21:8

The way of the guilty is devious, but the conduct of the innocent is upright.

Proverbs 21:18

The wicked become a ransom for the righteous, and the unfaithful for the upright.

Proverbs 21:29

A wicked man puts up a bold front, but an upright man gives thought to his ways.

Proverbs 28:10

He who leads the upright along an evil path will fall into his own trap, but the blameless will receive a good inheritance.

Proverbs 29:10

Bloodthirsty men hate a man of integrity and seek to kill the upright.

Proverbs 29:27

The righteous detest the dishonest; the wicked detest the upright.

PART EIGHT

Prosperity

GIVING

Proverbs 3:9, 10

Honor the LORD with your wealth, with the firstfruits of all your crops;

then your barns will be filled to overflowing, and your vats will brim over with new wine.

Proverbs 3:27, 28

Do not withhold good from those who deserve it, when it is in your power to act.

Do not say to your neighbor, "Come back later; I'll give it tomorrow"--when you now have it with you.

Proverbs 11:24

One man gives freely, yet gains even more; another withholds unduly, but comes to poverty.

Proverbs 11:25

A generous man will prosper; he who refreshes others will himself be refreshed.

Proverbs 19:6

Many curry favor with a ruler, and everyone is the friend of
a man who gives gifts.

Proverbs 21:26

All day long he craves for more, but the righteous give
without sparing.

Proverbs 22:9

A generous man will himself be blessed, for he shares his
food with the poor.

Proverbs 28:27

He who gives to the poor will lack nothing, but he who
closes his eyes to them receives many curses.

LAZINESS

Proverbs 6:6-8

Go to the ant, you sluggard; consider its ways and be wise!

It has no commander, no overseer or ruler,

yet it stores its provisions in summer and gathers its food at harvest.

Proverbs 6:9-11

How long will you lie there, you sluggard? When will you get up from your sleep?

A little sleep, a little slumber, a little folding of the hands to rest--

and poverty will come on you like a bandit and scarcity like an armed man.

Proverbs 10:4

Lazy hands make a man poor, but diligent hands bring wealth.

Proverbs 10:5

He who gathers crops in summer is a wise son, but he who sleeps during harvest is a disgraceful son.

Proverbs 10:26

As vinegar to the teeth and smoke to the eyes, so is a sluggard to those who send him.

Proverbs 12:24

Diligent hands will rule, but laziness ends in slave labor.

Proverbs 12:27

The lazy man does not roast his game, but the diligent man prizes his possessions.

Proverbs 13:4

The sluggard craves and gets nothing, but the desires of the diligent are fully satisfied.

Proverbs 15:19

The way of the sluggard is blocked with thorns, but the path of the upright is a highway.

Proverbs 18:9

One who is slack in his work is brother to one who destroys.

Proverbs 19:15

Laziness brings on deep sleep, and the shiftless man goes hungry.

Proverbs 19:24

The sluggard buries his hand in the dish; he will not even bring it back to his mouth!

Proverbs 20:4

A sluggard does not plow in season; so at harvest time he looks but finds nothing.

Proverbs 21:25, 26

The sluggard's craving will be the death of him, because his hands refuse to work.

All day long he craves for more, but the righteous give without sparing.

Proverbs 24:30-34

I went past the field of the sluggard, past the vineyard of the man who lacks judgment;

thorns had come up everywhere, the ground was covered with weeds, and the stone wall was in ruins.

I applied my heart to what I observed and learned a lesson from what I saw:

A little sleep, a little slumber, a little folding of the hands to rest--

and poverty will come on you like a bandit and scarcity like an armed man.

Proverbs 26:13, 14

The sluggard says, "There is a lion in the road, a fierce lion roaming the streets!"

As a door turns on its hinges, so a sluggard turns on his bed.

Proverbs 26:15

The sluggard buries his hand in the dish; he is too lazy to bring it back to his mouth.

Proverbs 26:16

The sluggard is wiser in his own eyes than seven men who answer discreetly.

PROSPERITY

Proverbs 3:13-16

Blessed is the man who finds wisdom, the man who gains understanding,

for she is more profitable than silver and yields better returns than gold.

She is more precious than rubies; nothing you desire can compare with her.

Long life is in her right hand; in her left hand are riches and honor.

Proverbs 8:14, 18-21

Counsel and sound judgment are mine; I have understanding and power.

With me are riches and honor, enduring wealth and prosperity.

My fruit is better than fine gold; what I yield surpasses choice silver.

I walk in the way of righteousness, along the paths of justice,

bestowing wealth on those who love me and making their treasuries full.

Proverbs 10:2

Ill-gotten treasures are of no value, but righteousness delivers from death.

Proverbs 10:3

The LORD does not let the righteous go hungry but he thwarts the craving of the wicked.

Proverbs 10:4

Lazy hands make a man poor, but diligent hands bring wealth.

Proverbs 10:15

The wealth of the rich is their fortified city, but poverty is the ruin of the poor.

Proverbs 10:22

The blessing of the LORD brings wealth, and he adds no trouble to it.

Proverbs 10:24

What the wicked dreads will overtake him; what the righteous desire will be granted.

Proverbs 11:4

Wealth is worthless in the day of wrath, but righteousness delivers from death.

Proverbs 11:28

Whoever trusts in his riches will fall, but the righteous will
thrive like a green leaf.

Proverbs 13:7

One man pretends to be rich, yet has nothing; another
pretends to be poor, yet has great wealth.

Proverbs 13:8

A man's riches may ransom his life, but a poor man hears
no threat.

Proverbs 13:11

Dishonest money dwindles away, but he who gathers
money little by little makes it grow.

Proverbs 13:22

A good man leaves an inheritance for his children's
children, but a sinner's wealth is stored up for the righteous.

Proverbs 14:20

The poor are shunned even by their neighbors, but the rich
have many friends.

Proverbs 14:24

The wealth of the wise is their crown, but the folly of fools
yields folly.

Proverbs 15:6

The house of the righteous contains great treasure, but the income of the wicked brings them trouble.

Proverbs 15:16

Better a little with the fear of the LORD than great wealth with turmoil.

Proverbs 15:17

Better a meal of vegetables where there is love than a fattened calf with hatred.

Proverbs 15:27

A greedy man brings trouble to his family, but he who hates bribes will live.

Proverbs 16:8

Better a little with righteousness than much gain with injustice.

Proverbs 17:1

Better a dry crust with peace and quiet than a house full of feasting, with strife.

Proverbs 18:11

The wealth of the rich is their fortified city; they imagine it an unscalable wall.

Proverbs 18:16

A gift opens the way for the giver and ushers him into the presence of the great.

Proverbs 18:23

A poor man pleads for mercy, but a rich man answers harshly.

Proverbs 19:4

Wealth brings many friends, but a poor man's friend deserts him.

Proverbs 19:14

Houses and wealth are inherited from parents, but a prudent wife is from the LORD.

Proverbs 20:21

An inheritance quickly gained at the beginning will not be blessed at the end.

Proverbs 21:6

A fortune made by a lying tongue is a fleeting vapor and a deadly snare.

Proverbs 21:17

He who loves pleasure will become poor; whoever loves wine and oil will never be rich.

Proverbs 22:4

Humility and the fear of the LORD bring wealth and honor
and life.

Proverbs 22:7

The rich rule over the poor, and the borrower is servant to
the lender.

Proverbs 22:16

He who oppresses the poor to increase his wealth and he
who gives gifts to the rich--both come to poverty.

Proverbs 23:4, 5

Do not wear yourself out to get rich; have the wisdom to
show restraint.

Cast but a glance at riches, and they are gone, for they will
surely sprout wings and fly off to the sky like an eagle.

Proverbs 24:3, 4

By wisdom a house is built, and through understanding it is
established;

through knowledge its rooms are filled with rare and
beautiful treasures.

Proverbs 27:24

For riches do not endure forever, and a crown is not secure
for all generations.

Proverbs 22:1

A good name is more desirable than great riches; to be
esteemed is better than silver or gold.

Proverbs 22:2

Rich and poor have this in common: The LORD is the
Maker of them all.

Proverbs 28:6

Better a poor man whose walk is blameless than a rich man
whose ways are perverse.

Proverbs 28:8

He who increases his wealth by exorbitant interest amasses
it for another, who will be kind to the poor.

Proverbs 28:10

He who leads the upright along an evil path will fall into his
own trap, but the blameless will receive a good inheritance.

Proverbs 28:11

A rich man may be wise in his own eyes, but a poor man
who has discernment sees through him.

Proverbs 28:13

He who conceals his sins does not prosper, but whoever
confesses and renounces them finds mercy.

Proverbs 28:19

He who works his land will have abundant food, but the one
who chases fantasies will have his fill of poverty.

Proverbs 28:20

A faithful man will be richly blessed, but one eager to get
rich will not go unpunished.

Proverbs 28:22

A stingy man is eager to get rich and is unaware that
poverty awaits him.

Proverbs 29:3

A man who loves wisdom brings joy to his father, but a
companion of prostitutes squanders his wealth.

Proverbs 30:8, 9

Keep falsehood and lies far from me; give me neither poverty nor riches, but give me only my daily bread.

Otherwise, I may have too much and disown you and say,
'Who is the LORD?' Or I may become poor and steal, and
so dishonor the name of my God.

STEWARDSHIP

Proverbs 10:4

Lazy hands make a man poor, but diligent hands bring wealth.

Proverbs 12:11

He who works his land will have abundant food, but he who chases fantasies lacks judgment.

Proverbs 12:27

The lazy man does not roast his game, but the diligent man prizes his possessions.

Proverbs 27:23, 27

Be sure you know the condition of your flocks, give careful attention to your herds;

You will have plenty of goats' milk to feed you and your family and to nourish your servant girls.

SURETY

Proverbs 6:1-5

My son, if you have put up security for your neighbor, if
you have struck hands in pledge for another,

if you have been trapped by what you said, ensnared by the
words of your mouth,

then do this, my son, to free yourself, since you have fallen
into your neighbor's hands: Go and humble yourself; press
your plea with your neighbor!

Allow no sleep to your eyes, no slumber to your eyelids.

Free yourself, like a gazelle from the hand of the hunter,
like a bird from the snare of the fowler.

Proverbs 11:15

He who puts up security for another will surely suffer, but
whoever refuses to strike hands in pledge is safe.

Proverbs 17:18

A man lacking in judgment strikes hands in pledge and puts
up security for his neighbor.

Proverbs 20:16; 27:13

Take the garment of one who puts up security for a stranger;
hold it in pledge if he does it for a wayward woman.

Proverbs 22:26, 27

Do not be a man who strikes hands in pledge or puts up
security for debts;

if you lack the means to pay, your very bed will be snatched
from under you.

WORK

Proverbs 6:6-8

Go to the ant, you sluggard; consider its ways and be wise!

It has no commander, no overseer or ruler,

yet it stores its provisions in summer and gathers its food at harvest.

Proverbs 10:4

Lazy hands make a man poor, but diligent hands bring wealth.

Proverbs 10:5

He who gathers crops in summer is a wise son, but he who sleeps during harvest is a disgraceful son.

Proverbs 10:16

The wages of the righteous bring them life, but the income of the wicked brings them punishment.

Proverbs 12:11

He who works his land will have abundant food, but he who chases fantasies lacks judgment.

Proverbs 12:14

From the fruit of his lips a man is filled with good things as surely as the work of his hands rewards him.

Proverbs 12:24

Diligent hands will rule, but laziness ends in slave labor.

Proverbs 12:27

The lazy man does not roast his game, but the diligent man prizes his possessions.

Proverbs 13:4

The sluggard craves and gets nothing, but the desires of the diligent are fully satisfied.

Proverbs 13:11

Dishonest money dwindles away, but he who gathers money little by little makes it grow.

Proverbs 14:23

All hard work brings a profit, but mere talk leads only to poverty.

Proverbs 16:3

Commit to the LORD whatever you do, and your plans will succeed.

Proverbs 16:26

The laborer's appetite works for him; his hunger drives him on.

Proverbs 18:9

One who is slack in his work is brother to one who destroys.

Proverbs 20:11

Even a child is known by his actions, by whether his conduct is pure and right.

Proverbs 21:25

The sluggard's craving will be the death of him, because his hands refuse to work.

Proverbs 22:29

Do you see a man skilled in his work? He will serve before kings; he will not serve before obscure men.

Proverbs 24:27

Finish your outdoor work and get your fields ready; after that, build your house.

Proverbs 27:18

He who tends a fig tree will eat its fruit, and he who looks after his master will be honored.

Proverbs 27:23, 27

Be sure you know the condition of your flocks, give careful attention to your herds;

You will have plenty of goats' milk to feed you and your family and to nourish your servant girls.

Proverbs 28:19

He who works his land will have abundant food, but the one who chases fantasies will have his fill of poverty.